BABY MAMMA DRAMA

Sean Timberlake

Printed in the United States of America

ISBN: 978-0-9720882-0-6

Now that I got myself nice and comfortable, I want to tell you a little story. It's based on some real issues that most people encounter on a day to day basis, but the twist is not getting caught up in this everyday bullshit, and being able to see this shit before it goes down, ya dig! And not only that, but move accordingly! "now that's some gangster shit, I said "can you, dig it "? I'm going to tell you about this kid I know! Now I'm going to tell you about my nigga cause I know this dude is one of the realest! Now, I'm not just trying to hype this shit up, cause I seen this shit with my own eyes, now bust it, everything this cat said he was going to do, "he did it"! And everybody most definitely did not know the type of shit this nigga had on his mind, or what he was capable of doing, but I know, cause most of the time he would tell me what he was about to do, when it was almost done, so I'm not really surprised but you might be! I seen this dude build houses, cars, start multiple businesses, travel the world , I mean really just do what ever he felt like doing, and still help a multitude of people, and stay REAL, truly amazing, defining all odds, never letting nothing,or no one stop his game,I'm proud to know this man, the way I do! This dude took some real issues, mixed them up with some hyp0rtheticals, accompanied with some real reports, of how it goes down in the courtroom, along with about 4 yrs. Of Jerry Springer, and Maury, on top of 15 yrs. In the barbershop and personal bull-shit that's been tried on him, my man, straight flipped the script, changed his whole purpose in life, and proved that the pen is mightier than the sword! The sword get you in trouble, the pen will get you paid, can you dig, that so buckle up, and watch your boy paint this here masterpiece! Yours truly, CAT!

I remember a part in the movie 48 Hrs. When Reggie

Hammon (played by Eddie Murphy) took Jack Cates badge and reminded him of what he told him his job consisted of, and that was bull-shit and experience ! Well come check out some of this bull- shit I had to experience, let's ride!

Beginning

Every word, in the contents of this book, is true; to the point if it were necessary, I would put my life up against the words herein. To the best of my recollection, I am writing each incident precisely and accurately. Some things you will read about, the average person would be ashamed of. Yet some of my experiences, one may very well be so proud of, or know someone that may have made it through such horrific ordeals. More times than none, the truth hurts so bad that people would rather stay in the state of denial, rather than to look in the mirror and face themselves, as well as some of their past actions. They would tend to choose their selective memory, meaning they would select what they would prefer to remember, rather than to deal with the truth, because the truth hurts and at times, real bad.

When you hurt someone emotionally, you hurt them very deep on the inside. Even though the victim my find it in their heart to forgive you, it is very hard to forget!

When pain is caused, whether it is physical, mental or emotional, it leaves a scar.

There is a true saying, "do unto others, as you would have them do unto you."

Very Special Thanks

To my entire staff; my lil brother Lamar, for all your help, support and loyalty.

To Mr. W. Johnson and Pattie McDaniels who gave me a chance and made it possible for me to receive my High School Diploma and participation in the Cosmetology Program.

The Reason My Book is Entitled
"Second Chance"

After reading, you can see for yourself that during my thirty-one years of life, I have encountered some very deadly, dangerous and disappointing experiences. I am fully aware that on numerous occasions my very existence could have been over. But for some reason, God allowed me to make it through. Therefore, I made the decision to at least try to make a difference with this new awareness!

Chapter One

Sean, or "Cat" as well call him, was two years old when he encountered his first experience with death. Sean was visiting his mother's twin sister's home, When he ran out into the street and was struck by a car. He was thrown approximately twenty feet into the air, his head was split opened and the ambulance driver told his father that he was dead. "No the hell he ain't," was his father's response. To this day, almost every time he is in his Uncle Junior's presence, he reminds him, "I breathed air back into your lungs boy."

In 1980, on the first day of school, at ten years old, Cat walked into his classroom and it seemed like everyone had on a pair of kangaroos, which was the most popular sneaker during that time. There were different styles. We like the little pocket that was on the side. He felt bad that he didn't have a par, so that night he asked his father if he would buy him a pair. When he told him how much they cost, the answer was no. They cost forty dollars at that time. Sean was mainly disappointed because he saw his father spend money on things that he felt wasn't important as a pair of sneakers for him. Cat's father provided for the family, but he just needed him to buy him a pair of kangaroos like his classmates.

The next day he was walking up the street and a lady who lived in the next block from him, asked him to go to the store and buy her a pack of cigarettes. She paid him a dollar. Cat began to think, adding In his head, "if forty people paid me a dollar for going to the store, I can buy my own Kangaroos". That day was the first day of his entrepreneurship.

Soon after that, he started going around to the Pleasantville Shopping Center, asking store owners if he could run errands, purchase lunch, ect; some hired him, some didn't. They saw the hustle in him and began asking him to do various odd jobs at their homes. He washed cars, cleaned yards, raked leaves, shoveled snow, or whatever to make money. The hustle was in him. This became his job after school, everyday, and he was very serious about making his own money. Sean kept his goal in mind, forty dollars a day. One day he met a lady named Ms. Effie Jenkins, who ran the zodiac record store, who, eventually becomes a very important figure in his life, in which you'll read about later. Sean began doing odd jobs for Ms Jenkins and her sister. One day he discovered another way to earn money. He began carrying bags for customers who shopped at Acme Supermarket, which was then located at the Shopping Center. I heard one person say "little man's trying to make some money;" and that I was. I earned anywhere from twenty-five cents to five dollars hustling at the Acme Supermarket. This went on for approximately three years. One day his older brother started coming around. He decided he was going to try to hustle a little; which was a problem at first because I wanted to make all the money myself, but after a while it was cool. Tony is fifty-one weeks older than Cat. He wouldn't do everything that Sean would do. As far as he was concerned, there was only "one him" out there, a natural hustler.

Cat and his brother used to fight a lot. If one of them just looked at the other one wrong, they were at each other like "cats and dogs". Most of the time tony would get his off first, and then Cat would leave the lasting impression, you know how it is with brothers. They had cousins who would play them against each other because they knew they were always fighting. You see the older

Timberlakes who grew up in the sixties and seventies, were known to be able to hold there own. They were rough; when you had a beef with one, you had to deal with twelve more. So I guess that's were the rough side of him comes from. Anyway, like I was saying, he and his brother fought a great deal. Their dad always appeared to be closer to Tony than Sean. He never could figure it out. Maybe it's the old "namesake syndrome". Whatever the reason. Cat always felt like an outcast. He was, and he still feels he is, very stubborn. He wouldn't cry when his day beat him. Tony always hollered like someone was killing him, and then when his dad go to him he wouldn't cry. "I don't know if it's my imagination but it always appeared as thought I got the harshest punishment" he said. As time went by, his heart became hardened and he became very rebellious and cold towards his dad. Years went by and Cat honestly felt like his dad didn't like him. Even though during this period of time in his life, he had these feelings toward his dad, life has a way of working things out. Sometimes a person will go full circle in their lifetime. He was then too young and immature to even think about or consider his ultimate destiny of life.

He was always into sports. At the e of eight years old, he began playing football for the Pleasantville Jokers. 1978 was the first year he played, in which he recalls weighing 55 lbs. He didn't even know anything about organized football; however, he was good and willing to learn the fundamentals of the game. He knew the object and was up on his moves, but he had one major handicap, his attitude. Later on in life, he learned that attitudes can play a large part in hindering one from success. Because of his attitude, smart mouth and bad temper, Sean was put on the list to be cut from the team. Fate had it so that the Head Coach, Mr. Richardson, was fond of him and saved him from being cut. In his position, he made the final decision. These were his exact words, "when you have a kid on the team this explosive, who knows the game, the moves, and is not scared, you don't cut him because of his attitude, you turn him into a football player!" He said, "He's small, but he has heart." That day, twenty-three years ago, Mr. Richardson gave Sean another chance.

He played ball from 1978 to 1984. His dad would come to some of his games. But a lot of times when he really needed him there, he wasn't. For instance; when Sean really had done and exceptional performance on the field, he needed him there to see him and give him praise. When some of the other players made a touchdown, Sean recalls seeing their parents running down the sideline rooting them on. I guess he needed that extra attention from his dad. He had a real struggle trying to obtain a relationship with his dad.

He continued with his everyday routine. By now he had "Mad Hustle" in him. I guess during this time in his life, the money had him. The more money he made, the more he wanted to make. He was able to buy the cloths he wanted, instead of what his parents wanted him to have. He had his own stash of foods and snacks he liked to eat. Capt'n Crunch was his favorite cereal. He kept his cereal, 2 liter bottles of soda and various cookies and candy in his room. I suppose he became too independent because one day his dad told him that he was going to the Shopping Center on his time, so he stopped him. His dad was trying to break him down because of his bad attitude problem. Different things began to go through his mind. He became more and more rebellious and can recall one incident that he held against his dad for a long time. His brother Tony was thirteen and their dad bought him a brand new Apache bike from Woolco for Christmas. He brought Sean a bike from a second hand store from a guy who rebuilt and painted bikes. You know, he fixed them up to make them look new. Cat didn't think that was right, so he bought him a racing bike, one that he put together himself. He bought a pooch frame and the other parts and built his own bike.

The year 1985, He was fourteen and a half, almost fifteen years old. He began noticing different things around him, things going on, just life in general. He was talking to one of his cousins one day and he told Cat that he was getting ready to buy some pot. he said "what's that weed?' He said, "Yeah." He lived in the suburbs. When he explained what he was buying and how much it was going to cost him, Cat asked him how he sold it. He told Sean that he broke it down into grams, that you get seven grams for thirty-five bucks. He went on to explain that you can break it down into seven grams and sell them for ten dollars each. Cat, being the math wizard that he is began figuring out that he would be doubling his money. So he made the decision right then and there and told his cousin that he wanted one. He hooked it up. He got the quarter and ended up bagging nine dimes out of it. He hung around the projects then. He burned it down and called his cousin the next day for two more of the same. Of course he was surprised that He had moved his supply so fast. He called his buddy and got a half ounce. By this time another cousin, who had been in and out of detention and county jail, was home from prison. Yafik and Cat was always cool, bust just coming home, he let me know that he was not trying to go back to prison. He was kind of hot headed. He would always come around our house for either a baseball bat or a golf club. One day Sean's dad wanted to know where all his golf clubs were because there were only three left in the caddy. Sean was on the block one day, business as usual, trying to get that paper, when Yafik recognized this cat that he referred to as "The Man." He told Cat that he sells coke and that it moves faster than weed. Little did Sean know that another big change was about to take place in his life.

He stepped to "The Man" and said, "yo my man, can I holler at you for a minute?" He looked at him and asked, "Who's this little guy?" Cat said, "I heard you're the man around here. I'm trying to get down with the coke game." "Who told you that shortie?" he asked. "You gone get me down or what?" he asked him. He gave Cat his number. He called him, and he wasn't lying. In that short time frame, from 1984 when he purchased that first weed package to 1985 when he was well into the coke scene, things had changed so fast that he had really lost control of his life. His whole life had turned for the worst during that time. Between 1984 and 1985, going into1986, the transition was so devastating; that either he or I can sit down and explain to you what actually happened to him. He was lost, completely out of control. Now when I look at the youth of today, in the age bracket he was in during that "Devastating time frame," of his life, He tries to do everything within his power to try to guide them in the right direction. During that time, he couldn't see himself so bad, yet he didn't have a clue as to where his life was headed. One day he sat down and deeply investigated his life. It was then that he began to focus on what he had to do to change his destiny.

When he changed his way of hustling into the illegal drug scene, of course that meant he needed a weapon. So he called another cousin who arranged for him to purchase a pistol. At fourteen years old, he had only had his pistol two or three months, before he caught his first gun charge. He and his brother stole some candy and took it to school to sell. They made one hundred fifty dollars and bought a moped. Cat was riding it one day with his gun on him, and got stopped. He had no license, no tags on the moped and a gun bulging in his front pocket. A cop pulled up behind him. When he asked him where he got the gun, Sean told him that he found it. He was taken to juvenile Court and placed on probation. But he couldn't stay out of trouble. He was too deep into the coke game.

In 1984 he finished playing with the jokers as the starting quarterback. All positions were open with the JV and Varsity Greyhounds Football Team at Pleasantville High School. There were two players who were two years ahead of him and they both transferred to other schools, therefore, Sean's chances looked promising for a position with the Greyhounds. One day Cat's mom decided to put them in a private school. Well, there went his chances for the greyhounds. He told his mom that the private school didn't have a football team, and she said they have a soccer team. He said, "mom, I play football." She told him that he had to play soccer. He tried to explain the difference, but mom wasn't hearing it. At the school, they had to explain why they wanted to go there and they had to tell them that they were born again Christians. His mom told them what they were supposed to say. From day one he was never comfortable there. He felt the staff; some of them anyway, were prejudice. They were there two and a half months before Sean got kicked out. His mom felt she should take them all out and keep the family together.

By the time Sean got back to Pleasantville High school, it was too late for the football team. He lost interest in everything. He just left school right after second period. Tarah his wife, enrolled at PHS. She was hanging with a girl Cat used to like in Junior High School. He'd see Tarah in the hallways with Iris and tease her, trying to get her attention. He'd do the dumb things kids do when they like a young lady, try to get her to pay for his lunch, jump in front of her in line, you know, stupid stuff. She wasn't interested; at least she said she wasn't. She was told that Sean was a lady's man. They did eventually end up together, breaking up a few times, but managed to work through their differences.

All through school, he never had a problem with rocking. If a joker wanted to get it on, they did what they had to do. There was this one kid from Newark named Malik. Since Junior High School, he and Cat had to fight every day. Ms Effie Jenkins saw and knew the road of trouble he was headed. She knew his family and he could feel general concerns she had for him. He began to loose focus in school. His attendance became bad he was on the verge of being thrown out of school. She told him that she was going to be running the Alternative School and offered to take him there, trying to prevent him from being kicked out of school. He didn't go right away, but he continued his bad habits. The guidance office called him down one day and informed that if he missed another day or got into another fight, he was going to be expelled. He didn't care because he knew Ms. Effie Jenkins cared, so he went to the Alternative School. The mentality he was in back then, blows my mind because it seems as though, he was just existing.

He didn't have to be in school until two o'clock in the afternoon, so that made it easy for him to continue his lifestyle of running the streets. He had become very bold with his activities. He'd stay out until one, two, and sometimes three o'clock in the morning. There were times he'd just get a hotel room instead of going home because he didn't want his mom to see him in the condition he was in. He stayed high or drunked up. When I tell you that he was out of control, that's putting it lightly.

One of his partners in Alternative school had a beef with this cat from another city and they had words between each other on this particular day. They let him go then, but they ran into him later on that night at the projects. They decided they had to run down on him, so as soon as they saw him, Sean whipped out his pistol. He ran across the street with Cat's partner beating him down. He had taken the pistol from Sean and smacked this cat a few times with it. In street talk, we smashed him straight out. The kid ran down the street and I don't think it was more than a minute later before police were everywhere. He had told five O that they pistol whipped him. Sean couldn't believe that cat did that. He wasn't used to being ratted on.

There was a young lady He was seeing at the time, whose aunt lived nearby, so he ran over there, loaded with drugs. During all the excitement, somehow, the gun had been passed from Cat's partner to his lady, and she then passed it to his partners cousin, who lived way over on the other side of the projects. Five O had a manhunt out them, which at the time was approximately ten o'clock pm. The decided to lay low and left about one o'clock a.m. He and his lady friend were walking up Adams Avenue when five O ran down on them. Cat threw the drugs and the gun. The police took him past his house to let his parents know they were taking him to the police station for questioning. They had his partner there in another room questioning him. They asked Sean what happened and where the gun was. Of course he told them that he didn't know. They brought this one detective in, who Sean had knew had a big problem with him. He informed him on more than one occasion that he was going to nail him. Looking back on that time of his life, he was his worst nightmare. This detective had been watching him for more than two years. He had stopped him a couple of times when he was loaded with money, with all his jewelry on, not realizing that he was setting his self up, or the picture he was painting of himself for the police. The detective had a partner Cat called Uncle. He was always in his real uncle's store and at the Shopping Center. He knew him since his youth, however, once he was In the streets, he knew he was on one side of the law and uncle was on the other side. He warned him often that he'd better get off the block. He was stubborn and hardheaded and did not want to hear anything Uncle had to say. He saw him as his enemy.

There was a particular white detective, who they heard was a racist. He did a lot of dirty stuff. He made it his business to get to the station when he heard Sean was there. He told him, "If that boy picks your picture in a photo lineup, I promise you, you're going to jail tonight." He had him in a backroom. He heard a lot of hollering in the next room. He heard the officer saying, "You're lying. You're eighteen; I just talked to your father. You're going to the county tonight." They kept them in separate rooms, interrogating them. Cat kept telling them that he didn't know what they were talking about. Once they brought them in the same room, and Cat's partner winked at him. When he did that, he felt he was letting him know that they didn't know anything. He was getting real tired. It was late, but he knew if he gave in, the charges would be that much more because drugs were with the gun. They told him, "You may as well give us the gun." But he was too stubborn to give in. After approximately three more hours of interrogation, they were charged with Aggravated Assault, Terroristic Threats, Possession of a handgun, Possession of a handgun with intent and Conspiracy, Five charges.

He was sent to Harbor fields Juvenile Facility. This was his first time actually being locked up. The police tried to pump it up to be so bad, but when he got there, it didn't seem to be as they had said. I'm not trying to say its okay by no means, because just having your freedom taken away from you, is not a good feeling. Once you're a part of the "system" you're owned by the "system." Even though it didn't seem as bad as he thought it would be, He also knew that if something jumped off, he would have to handle his business.

Now his mom had a little hustle in her too. During that time, she had a little side business cleaning houses. She worked for very reputable people in the area, doctors, Lawyers, Casino Presidents and various Business Owners. Yeah, you guessed it; His mom was able to retain a top notch attorney from one of the largest law firms in the area at that time. One of the first things his attorney asked was if his partner had signed anything? He told them no. He then asked him if he was sure. Of course he had no idea that his trusted partner was willing to sell him out. One day Cat ran into his partner, who had just gotten out of the County Jail on bail. He asked him if he had told the authorities anything. He said "no Sha." Sharif was his street name. Soon after that day, he found out differently. When he went to his Lawyers office, he showed him a signed statement by his "former" partner. He had sold Cat out to the prosecutor. At an early age, he learned a good lesson, that you can't trust anybody. He had heard an alleged story about these two guys from Atlantic City who had gotten jammed up in a situation. Supposedly, a teacher had hit one of them and he got a gun from the other one. He then went to the teacher's home and blasted him away. They both got extensive time for the incident.

After being at the Harbor Fields Juvenile Facility for two weeks, Cat shipped out to Mercer County, which was unusual. For some reason this is what happened, and later he realized, at that time, he was given another chance. The actual court hearing was held in Mercer County. He was told that he could get ten to fifteen years, even though the real story was that his partner had taken the gun out of his hand. The table turned to look as if he had performed the whole crime alone. With the extent of the charges imposed on him, people could not believe that he was only put on house arrest. The conditions of his sentence were that he was only to leave the house for work or school. Well, he was trying to hustle while being on house arrest. The police were watching him big time. Cat had guys on the block for him and others doing this and that, just handling his business, so he thought. The chicks were big on him they'd look out for him. They would hold his pistol and drugs for him. Tara was still in the picture, on and off. She couldn't run the streets, not to say she was willing to, but she was his heart.

One of the girls came down to meet him at the Alternative school one day. They were walking down Main street, when, wouldn't you know his favorite detective passed by. I'll never forget the look he gave me, a look that said, "I'm coming to get you," He had a quarter of an ounce on him. He didn't turn around, but asked his girl if he stopped. She turned and looked and said, "no, but you know he's coming back." Before she could get the words out, he had the coke in her bra and snatched her across the street in a Barber shop. He told her to go into the bathroom and stay there. She hid the drugs in there and came out. He was seated like he was waiting for a haircut with his headset on his ears. Five O came in the back door. One of the officers said, "Stand up and take the headset off." Cat looked at him and said, "I can hear you, I don't have to take the headset off." The arrogance and disrespect for them was so obvious. Uncle showed up. There were approximately six to seven police officers. Sean's girl just stood there with her arms folded. You know, as if to say, "I ain't going nowhere." The sisters know how to be sarcastic and get there message across. Uncle took the headset off his head. He in turn, held the walkman up and then dropped it on the floor. Then just looked at him as if to ask, "and what?"

They never touched him, however, they told him to step outside. He always carried a bag of candy in his pocket, Five O told him to take everything out of his pockets. He had his candy and a large bankroll. They just looked at him. They then told him to put the money on the ground. He put the money on the ground, but decided to pick it back up. They told him again to put the money on the ground. He did, but put his foot on it. They told him to move his foot and he asked "for what?" Then they had him to pull his pockets inside out. He asked them if they had a search warrant. Uncle and the other detective looked at each other. They knew they were illegally searching him. I guess he was a little too smart for them, because they then told him to pick the money up, open the car door, and put his hands on the headrest and slide all the way to the other side of the car. He was never handcuffed, He wasn't read his rights and they did several things that they were not supposed to do, therefore, he really didn't have to go with them. It was some time later that he realized it though. He got into the car as they told him and went to the Police Department. I believe they thought Uncle could talk to him and he would cooperate with them. He had already realized which team Uncle was on. What he saw was that Uncle was not trying to help him. that he was trying to get him locked up; He saw him trying to help his boys.

Uncle said to him, "Sean, I'm going to call your father and get permission to strip search you." He said to him, "I get one phone call, and I want to call my lawyer. He learned fast.

They asked him where he got the money. He told them, "from my girl who works in the casino." Their reply was, "good answer," but you could almost feel steam coming from their faces. They were hot. He could hear others going through his bag of candy. They actually went through every piece, unwrapping and trying to rewrap it, looking for drugs. He knew they wanted him bad, but he was a hard one for them. Cat was given his bag of candy back; some pieces still had paper off. He laughed and threw the bag in the trash they wouldn't let his girl come to the Police Station, so she went back to the Barber Shop, got the drugs she stashed, and hit the streets.

Sean's father came to the Police department. He asked if they had found anything. They said no. Sean was sixteen years old, and that was the first time he heard his dad stand up for him. "I'm tired of you harassing my son," he said. "You didn't find anything and you just keep stopping him for no reason. If you catch him wrong, then he's wrong. You can't keep stopping him for no reason," his dad told them.

Uncle said, "Tony, your son is out on these streets and he's going to get himself in trouble."

Things weren't looking too good for him. He was back and fourth in court. One day his lawyer told him that his partner testified against him. He was forced to make a deal with the prosecutors office. He could have gotten three to five years for the gun charge alone because he did take part in the incident. He didn't do all the things his former partner's statement said he did, but when you make a deal, you're saying you did just what those papers say you did. He ended up with a four to six month program out of Jamesburg. After the court hearings, he had to wait a month for his sentencing date, which was scheduled for June 9th. They were giving him the opportunity to finish out the year in Alternative school.

Cat and his brother used to frequently visit their cousin Sean in Baltimore. He was older than them, but he was living a lifestyle past his peers anyway, therefore age really didn't matter me him. On ne of his trips to Baltimore, Sean meets a girl from Princeanne, MD. So he gave her a call and told her that he wouldn't be seeing her for awhile, but he'd write her. She knew right away that something was wrong, and that he was going to jail. Her first instinct was that he had shot someone, because she knew he carried a gun. She told him she was graduating that week so he promised her he would be there. A friend of his was going with him, but he let him down at the last minute. Now keep in mind that Sean was on house arrest, and preparing to go out of state. He packed cloths for a few days along with his pistol. He learned later that his mom was panicking and was almost ready to call Five O and report him missing. "When I think back, I was very selfish. It was all about me. I didn't care who I hurt, in fact, I just wasn't thinking much at all." He recalls.

So he made the trip to Maryland, alone. No brother with him, not even his cousin. He got a hotel room feeling really uncomfortable, probably because he knew he wasn't supposed to be there anyway. He was in a strange city, clubbing, partying and stressing. He had the strangest experience to happen to him that week-end. H had gone out of his room one night to get something to drink and there was a couple registering for a room. They had another female waiting in the car who yelled something to him, showing an interest in wanting to come to his room. So he hollered his room number to her. He just couldn't let her play him out, you know, the man thing. About twenty minutes later, he heard a knock on his door. He looked through the peephole ant saw it was her. So he let her in. She was running off at the mouth. Of course he didn't have much conversation. He asked her what she was doing that night, and she proceeded to tell him what she was going to do to him. Cat realized he didn't have any rubbers, so he told her that he had to run down to the corner store and he'd be right back. He hid his jewelry, put his pistol where he could get to it and left her there until he got back. That was the wildest thing he ever thought of doing. He made it back home without any occurrences. He had left for Maryland on a Thursday on the bus,, came back on Monday and went to court for sentencing on Tuesday.

He ended up doing five months. He was sent to Sandy Hook Residential Youth Facility. Here they looked and acted like grown men because of the street experiences they had. Sean became close to this cat they called K Love from Neptune. There was another cat they called Mont Mont Davis from Long Branch who said to him one day, "I hear you're from Pleasantville where things are real pleasant." Sean said something slick back to him like, "everything ain't pleasant in Pleasantville, but whatever." He said, "you said that like you're tough or something." Sean replied, "Tough enough." They were beefing for a minute but eventually Mont and Sean became real cool.

He met another cat named Stacy Richardson, Stay U, from East Orange. He was a thorough cat, Sean didn't know much about him when he first got there, but he soon found out that they were scared to death of him. It was Cat's first time down and those guys like to play games when you were kind of new to things. One day this cat was talking real slick to him and he was talking slick back to him. Everybody was looking, you know, because they knew how this cat operated, and most of them was scared of him. They were thinking, this cat is crazy. Cat was new and didn't really know his reputation yet. He had banged a couple of cats up in there, but that didn't really matter to him. So because he stood up to him, he asked Sean if he wanted to go in the back. Most of the time if you're asked in the back or in a cats room, he'll want to get something off his chest' it's time to put some work in you. So he went in the back, and he looked at Cat with gangster eyes and asked, "What's up?" Cat said, "What's happening brother?" He said, "listen man, this is your first time down?" He said, "Yeah, well I was in Harbor Fields before for a couple of months, but this is my first time in a joint like this." He said, "shortie, your crazy, man. When somebody says they want to go in the back, they want to fight." Cat looked at him and said, "you want to fight me?" He said, "No shortie, go head, but look you gotta keep your eyes open on what's going on. I don't know if you're real or not but most of these guys are scared to death of me." He laughed it off and said, "You're alright shortie." Now this guy was in Cat's group. They had a lot of privileges, for instance, they could go to Great Adventure when they wanted to. All they had to do was write a plan, kick it out and vote on it as a group. Say U had a plan of being released. He worked up a proposal for his release home. They told him that everybody in the group had to vote. They all thought he was crazy. There was a murder in Stay U's eyes when Cat was approached because he didn't vote in his favor. He said to Cat that he thought they were alright. He told him they are but he felt as though the counselors would feel they were just skating people through if he voted in his favor because of the fact that he was only one and a half weeks into the program. He also felt it wouldn't be fair because he didn't know him; Cat didn't even know why U was there. He told him that he never heard him kick anything out in the group. After bringing all this to his attention he thought about it.

Stay U did get his release but he was injured pretty bad. He got caught in a crossfire, messing him up pretty bad. They were relieved to know he made it. Cat heard a lot about him after he left. Whether he realized it or not, his friend Stay U also got a second chance.

He was warded the opportunity to learn a few skills while housed at Sandy Hook. They fixed up an old house and he realized that one can obtain quite a bit of knowledge by just watching, or even just putting in a helping hand. He learned a little about electrical work and different tools, receiving a certificate upon completion.

Chapter Two

The day came sooner than he thought for his release from Sandy Hook. One day out of the blue, he was asked how he felt about going home. I don't think I have to say how he felt inside. Just the thought of freedom felt so good. Of course he thought they were kidding when he was told that they were preparing to put him on a train to go home. When he called his father and told him, he was shocked at his reaction. He told him that he was coming right away to pick him up. That was the first time his father said something to make him think he really loved him. It meant so much to him the way he just stepped up to the plate, so to speak. Sean's dad showed up with Cousin Benny and Cousin Punkin.

All he could think about was his girl Tara. She stood by him while he was away with food packages and different things. He wanted to make peace with her and to be with her. She just told him that she would be there for him. The plan was that he would return to school, but of course that didn't happen. He hit the streets again.

One of his partners tried to spare him. He knew the game out on the streets was different from when he was away just those few months. There were numerous drug busts, their peers getting gunned down, some shot and dumped in wooded areas, and yet others hog-tied in their cars and killed. His man told him he'd take care of him, that he'd give him some money to hold him until he got straight. But Cat was never one to take from anyone.

He was his own man, so he thought. Sean just told his partner he was cool. But they all knew his potential for "getting that paper."

So here he is, out on the streets again, only two days after his release. He knew pop o was lurking around, but that didn't stop him. He told this one guy he needed something to get him on his feet. He gave Cat three and a half grams, but it was cut. He had it bagged and sold in two hours. He ran the transaction down to his man Sheed, who stepped to him about it, but his answer was he must have given him the wrong package. Sheed says to him," I don't want you out here anyway." The guy that gave him the package, made good for it and threw in some extra. He was scared to death of Sheed. One thing Cat was always on the move, never staying in one place too long. He left Sheed's house, with three and a half grams of coke on him and approximately two hundred twenty-five dollars in his pocket that he had just made in only twenty minutes. He spotted po po, they were everywhere. He recalls thinking, "oh my god, I'm going back." Po Po had raided the projects, and was probably watching this one guy in particular, because they went right over to him. Cat had nothing to loose and nowhere at all to run, so he just walked right passed them while they were getting out of their cars. Once he got across the street, he broke. He ran to sheed's house banging on the door. He knew something was wrong, so he answered the door with his pistol in his hand. He said, "See you're hardheaded, hardheaded." He got up out of that one, another chance.

The close call with the law still did not stop him from doing what he felt he had to do. It was like an addiction. He was home for only two days, and so close to returning to lockup. He was sixteen years old, had a little training, headed in the right direction, yet found himself in the midst of all that drama. With police lights flashing everywhere and knowing what could happen to him in one split second, he still returned to the life that could ultimately destroy him. He just shook it off and went right back to it, only this time, even more aggressively. He began making trips to New York and Philadelphia with his partner, who was crazier than he was. He was down with "whatever." They made more money, being their "own boss." Their girls were related so they hung out quite a bit together. They went out to the finest restaurants, ordering Lambrusco Chella, Moet, Steak, Lobster and you name it. Cat became wilder and looser by the day, becoming more comfortable with the game, and of course carrying his pistol at all times. His pistol was part of his dress code, strapping it on as if he was putting on his underwear. His mother was so afraid for him. She knew he was involved in something, but she wasn't, at that time, street smart. She would ask him, "son, what are you involved with in the streets?" He didn't want to hurt her, although he knew he was. He loved his mother very much, but he was blind.

During the next few years, between '87 and '89, the streets were very dangerous in south Jersey. It became very serious out there, the wildest times in the area, until the later part of '99 to '2000. He lost quite a few friends and acquaintances due to murders in the streets. They were being tracked down and murdered wherever they were caught. Death was al around, and looking back, He can't see how he didn't think it could happen to him. But when you're caught up in the game, you never think it could happen to you. During that time, if you didn't strap up, you were done one way or another, robbed or killed. On several occasions he was warned that there were those who wanted to stick him up. One day he was warned that there was a guy who wanted to rob him.

Since they had the same first cousin, they had family ties, so Sean ignored the threat. Cat and his partner were at the projects one day, just chilling and listening to his police scanner, you know, keeping up with the Po Po. He always tried to know where they were at all times, just like they wanted to know where he was. They did some dirty things at times, like throwing down drugs on the ground, and putting them in your pocket; you got beat up, and all kinds of dirty things, therefore, He tried to stay prepared. He'd slip into someone's house when they showed up. Well this cat had his partner lure Cat's partner away as he walked up beside him, talking to him at the same time. The next thing you know, he stepped behind Cat and put him in a sleep hold. He hit his pockets, and then he slapped him and hit him on the head a few times. He woke up trying to chase him but he got dizzy. He got him for eight or nine hundred dollars that day. I don't know if it was on purpose or not but he dropped his police scanner.

Cat's partners wanted to handle the situation for him. They couldn't understand why he wouldn't let it go down the way they wanted it to. They said, "Somebody has to pay." Sean had to let them know that he was related. They still asked what he wanted to do about it, talking some crazy talk. He just told them not to worry about that, he would take care of it. He just let that one ride. A lot of times we do things without thinking. Thank God as far as that particular situation was concerned, he thought about the actions he was going to take and also about the circumstances that would follow his actions. Many an innocent bystander or family member is hurt or even killed behind someone's stupidity. In our culture it is not, or even was a normal thing to harm someone's relative because of a problem one may have with another. I cannot understand how anyone can take someone else's life and live with it the rest of his or her life. Back in the day, there were rules. Today the rules are broken because you'll have someone to testify right in front of you in court, even lie. Gangster stuff is going on now. When the pressure is on and you have cops in your face telling you you're facing twenty, ten, or five years, a cat will start singing and begin telling on everybody. That type of pressure make a cat fold up like a dollar bill. Sean had a couple of jokers tell on him one time. The pressure was on, they couldn't take it, so they talked.

The same year, a couple of months prior, Cat had a cousin to tell him he was in need of seven hundred dollars until next month. He told him he had a half ounce he could let him sell and he would make about four hundred dollars. He was down for it; however Cat knew he had no prior experience in the streets. So he arranged for one of his partners to move the package for him, trying to help him out. One day I guess his cousin thought he'd try to help him out by telling him he had a friend that wanted half. Sean called his partner LT and the three of them went over the city. He said this girl that he worked with, who lived in the mission, wanted some coke. He took them to a parking lot and called her. She said she would be there in five minutes, but never showed. Cat asked him if he thought this friend of his was setting them up. He assured Sean that she wouldn't do anything like that. After awhile, Cuz got out of the car and walked toward the church. When he got to an alley, he saw Po Po, so he panicked and ran back to the car. It turned out that Po Po was looking for some dude who had beat up his girlfriend and her one year old daughter. They thought my cousin was they guy they were looking for, so they came after us, chasing us out of the parking lot onto North Carolina Avenue. A light turned yellow and Sean yelled, "Don't stop." They came to a red light and he told Cuz to take it, but he said no and put on brakes. He was worried about his car.

Knowing Po Po was on their a**, and he was real dirty, Cat started stuffing his underwear with the drugs. Just as Cuz slammed on the brakes, the police pulled up beside them and had a pencil in his face, ordering, "pull the m*****f******* car over before I blow your m*****f****** brains out." At least five additional police cars were now on the scene. With all his involvement in the streets, this was his first time in an actual scene such as this. One by one they were all pulled out of the car with weapons drawn on them. The Sergeant pulled up and asked, "Is he over there?" One of the officers responded by saying, "no, unless he grew hair instantly." That let us know that the guy they were looking for was bald. It was wintertime with snow on the ground, and they had hats on, so they possibly would have been released with a summons if Cuz hadn't reacted the way he did towards the officers. Later Cat found out that Cuz was intoxicated and that was the reason for his behavior. What transpired next was far worse than the Rodney king incident.

They sat them outside the car and then they were questioned. One of the officers asked Cat's cousin why he ran. He gave them some sorry excuse, but they weren't having it. They were seventeen years old and Cuz had a brand new Nissan, insured, tagged, all legal, and the car was in his name, however he only had a stamped permit. They ran LT's name and it came up with a warrant. The officer said, "Put your hands behind your back, you're under arrest." LT looked at Cat, but the look on his face let him, know that he was not surprised. The next thing they knew, Cuz had walked around the car and asked one of the officers, "May I ask what you're doing in my car?" The officer replied, "you get the f*** away from the car before I beat you're a** out here." Cuz said, "f** you b***, this is my car." The cop stood up and asked, "oh yeah?" At the same time he was walking toward him with a flashlight in his hand that he had pulled out of his pocket, slapping Cuz in the face with it. Then he began to just bash him in the face over and over. Sean said, "oh my God." He really couldn't believe what he was witnessing out there. His cousin couldn't have weighed more than ninety pounds soaking wet with bricks in all four pockets. "My father's going to kill you," he screamed. "I can't believe you're doing this to me." Cat hollered at him, "shut up, just shut up." He knew he was only making things worse for himself by running off at the mouth. There were five, maybe six officers literally whipping his a**. He was really beat down bad. Later Sean found out that Cuz thought the police were cutting his seats open, and that's the reason why he came around the other side of the car.

After a few minutes Cat couldn't take anymore. He started toward them saying, "why you gotta?' Before he could finish, another cop came up behind him and said, "They'll do the same thing to you." So he hollered to him one more time, "yo Cuz, just shut up."

Those five or six police officers, all weighing over two hundred pounds and every bit of six feet tall, were all on Cat's cousin for at least five minutes. Blood was everywhere.

Now there was also a woman watching the whole thing from across the street. So she decides to intervene. She said, while starting across the street, "I can't sit here and watch you beat him like that. "One of the officers said, "b****, you'd better go back before you get some of this too." This is an example of the dirty stuff I've seen the law do to people. If they had to beat him, which they didn't, and wasn't supposed to anyway, why not just one of them?

After they were finished beating up Cat's cousin, they began to think about the possibility that they must have something to hide. They decide to search the car and they found twelve bags of coke wrapped up in a piece of paper torn out of a magazine. One of the cops started laughing and said, "I have a funny question, whose is this?" Of course no one spoke up. "Just what I thought," he said. "It's everybody's." Cat looked at LT, he was already headed for jail, however, he had intentions of bailing him right out. He had put the drugs under Sean's seat, and he had all his drugs in his underwear. Cat looked right at him as if to ask, nigga you ain't gonna say nothing? He wouldn't open his mouth. They handcuffed Cuz making them so tight that they cut his wrist, and then they raised his arms toward his head to cause additional pain. That day they witnessed, "Dirty Cops" in action. You see it on TV, and believe me, it's for real; but not all of them are dirty.

When they walked into the Police Department, the first person they saw was the lady who witnessed the beating. She started mouthing, "call me a b**** now, beat me up now like you said you were going to do." they down played it, you know with the "officer's code." They told her that there was nothing they could do for her complaint then, but if she wanted to come back the next day, she could contact Internal Affairs. I don't know how far that lady took her actions, but just possibly, she was Cat's Guardian Angel that day, just based on the outcome of their arrest, which you'll read about later.

Cuz was still running off at the mouth. He told them he was eighteen years old, which put him in lock-up on the adult side. Cat was locked up on the juvenile side. Because he was still flapping his lips, he got punched in the face again while handcuffed to the wall.

Approximately forty-five minutes later, they found out

Cuz was a juvenile also, and that of course, made them nervous. When they brought him around to the juvenile side, he came in very upset accusing him, "it's all your fault we're in here." he was ready to blackout on him, but he kept his cool. The fact still remained, he took they to the city, he's the one who ran, he wouldn't listen when he told him to run the red light, he started running off at the mouth when they were probably going to be released with a summons, but instead of home, they were going to Harbor Fields. They began asking him why he had so many credit cards. They ran a check, none of them were stolen and all of them were in his name. Cuz looked at Cat and said, "I can't go to Harbor Fields. I've got to go to work tomorrow morning." He told him they didn't care about his job. He said, " I can't go to jail." He could tell Cuz was terrified. That was a prime example of a kid, with little or no knowledge of the streets, whose life was about to go completely in a different direction.

They were taken to Harbor Fields. Cat knew the set up there, how you were processed through the system. He planned out how he was going to smuggle the drugs, he managed to keep in his underwear, into Harbor Fields Juvenile Detention Center. They started asking him questions and after a few minutes, he asked to go to the bathroom. He stashed the drugs and went back for a final questioning. After he was strip searched, he slipped around and picked up his drugs, then bounced to his room. He had forty, twenty bags on him. He told the guard it was his cousins first time being locked up and asked if he could be in the room with him. "I don't think he can survive in here alone because he's not jail material," he told the guard. They agreed to let him room with Sean.

They were there about a month and a half. One day Cuz told him that he wanted to kill himself. He said to him, "little Cuz, while we are here, it's my job to protect you, and I'm not going to let anything happen to you." He got loose after Cat had that talk with him.

I guess he felt safe then.. A couple of times Sean had to beat him down, work him over a little. One time Cat walked in when he was on the phone with his mother. He heard him tell her that it was all Sean's fault. He hauled off and slapped him. For years his aunt blamed him totally for their lock-up, and to this day, I don't think he ever came clean with her. Over and over Sean found himself going back down because of trying to help someone, always getting caught up in a web. Yet if he didn't, he was considered the bad guy. Cat was in lock-up for beating up his cousin. The guard asked Cuz if he wanted to go back in the room with him or with someone else, he told him with him. Cuz was really scared that he was going to be sent to Jamesburg, but Cat knew he would most likely get probation. He told him, "lets just wait it out, and if I have to, I'll take all the weight." Even though he seemed to be in agreement with what he said, one day he saw him sitting in the room looking up at the vent in the wall. He asked him what was wrong, and he told him that he can't go to the Burg (meaning Jamesburg). He said, "if they send me to the burg, I'm going to kill myself." He asked him, "you want to die nigga? You ain't gotta kill yourself, let me do it for you." While he was snapping on him, he was hitting him with some serious body shots. He wouldn't fight back, instead he curled up in a fetal position. Sean told him, "That's what happens in real jails. Keep your moth shut until we go to court."

While there at Harbor fields, he remembers asking his mother to bring him some sneakers and a few other things from the house. Of course she brought the wrong pair. The guard called his mother to the bathroom and showed her what she discovered. His mother had brought the sneakers that were full of empty coke bags stuffed inside. He recalls that same guard looking up his nose. She said, "all your nose hair is gone, do you know what you're doing to yourself?" No, he didn't realize what he was doing, but he could imagine where he'd be today if he stayed on that same path of life.

One day, while still at Harbor Fields, a Spanish guy, who was visiting another Spanish guy there at the time, came up to him and told him he heard he had some coke. He told Sean if he gave him some, they would be alright. He knew that meant he wouldn't snitch. The one that was locked up had mad drugs coming in to him, heroin, and the whole nine yards.

When they went before the judge, everything seemed to have been in their favor. First of all, the defense attorney argued that he couldn't see why five two hundred pound, six feet tall police officers had to arrest this ninety-seven pound juvenile. Their explanation for all the bruises and marks sustained from the beating, was that Cuz slipped on ice. The case ended up being thrown out of court. The judge dismissed the case. Sean couldn't help thinking about the woman who stood watching when his cousin was being beat up by those five officers, and then showed up at the police department before they even got there. Later in life's experiences he would learn how God will use anything or anybody in order to intercede for you. Need I say, he was given another chance. Sometime later, during that same year, this cat from AC, A big dope boy, started doing kind of bad. He was known to get major paper. Cat wanted to make a trip to NY, and couldn't go on that day, so he told him that he needed four ounces right away, for a day or two. A friend of Sean's, Fahey, warned him not to mess with him. He told Cat that he and his boys would try to rob him,. He said, "he ain't gonna rob me. Fahey said, "word is bond they're gonna try to rob you." Cat set up a meeting at the projects. He called him at 10:00, but he wasn't ready yet. He told Sean to call him back in an hour. He called him back at 11:00, but he still wasn't ready. He told him to call him back in another hour, so he called him at 12:00, and he told him to meet him in forty-five minutes in the back of the projects. His brother Tony and his partner Nasheed were with him that night. Now it was ironic that his brother had a ford escort, two toned brown, just like the one he had the previous year. They all went around to the projects, his brother stayed in the car. AZ pulled up in a jeep, not realizing his brother was sitting inside the car. Cat walked over to the jeep, and he said, "get in." Sean got in and he put the jeep in reverse. Sean said, "ho, ho, what are you doing?" He told him that he didn't bring it with him, and that they had to go get it. Cat said, "no, hold up." He then said, "your man can come too" So he opened the door and yelled for his partner to come on. Nasheed walked over, walking slow, with heavy boots on and hands in his pockets. AZ said, "What's up?" Nasheed said, "What's up?" (That was the slang back then) Sheed got into the jeep and he proceeded to pull across the street and out onto Mulberry Avenue. He then dipped real quick, put the vehicle in park, jumped out and ran across the street. He had a blazing system in the jeep, so Cat turned the music up and was chilling, when all of a sudden, Sheed whipped out his pistol, touched him on the arm with it and said, "man, something ain't right." He said to him, "what's up man, you bugging." He said again, "something ain't right." Cat said, "Man, chill out." Then turned the music down, looking over his left shoulder, and just as he turned back around completely, he peeped in the rear view mirror and spotted this guy creeping up on the side of the jeep with a pistol in his hand. He saw it wasn't AZ, but before either one of them could react, he had the pistol in his face, telling him to move over. Cat got out of the jeep, stood next to him and said, "what's up?" He said, "get the f*** back in the jeep." Cat said to him, "nigga, you get in the back. "I don't know how he was thinking, or if he was thinking at all, because this cat had a gun on him, and he didn't even have his in his possession. He got in and put his pistol in his waistband. He thought Sheed was going to hit him right then, but he just climbed over the seat to get out and the guy grabbed him, but Sheed pulled his arms out of the coat, showing the pistol in his hand, so he let him go. AZ and his partner had a plan, and it was just as Fahey had warned him, they had planned to rob him, maybe even kill him. Their plan was deterred because he was supposed to be alone, and I do believe if they knew Sean's brother Tony was in the car, they would have gone back to him, for revenge. See, the fact that Tony had a car like the one Cat used to have, made them think it was his car out there. Tony was in the car sleep, not knowing anything that transpired out there.

They bounced over to Sheed's house on the other side of the projects, put on their sweathoods and grabbed another pistol. Sheed's sister saw everything. She asked them what was going on. Sheed told her to stay in the house and not to come outside. They then ran across the field, jumped over the fence, not knowing if AZ and his partner were still around. The car wasn't moved, therefore, they thought they were probably still in the area. They were planning to sneak up on them. By now Cat was real mad, especially knowing his brother was in the car sleeping. His adrenalin was pumping and he was thinking to himself, "if they do anything to my brother, I'll kill 'em." They ran down the expressway fence lane, looking around, but see nobody. Sheed covered him while he jumped over the fence, then he covered Sheed while he jumped over the fence. They were acting like they were on some real swat type s***, like we were specially trained for this type of action. Everything looked clear, so they went back over to the car. The windows were steamed up. They threw a couple of rocks on the car, trying to wake Tony. Finally, he popped his head up, asking them what was going on. Cat hollered, "just drive the car." He didn't know AZ's partner, but he did get a good enough look at him to know who he is if he ever saw him again. The wipers weren't clearing the windows fast enough, so they opened the windows, Sheed whipped out his pistol when he saw a blurred shape coming toward them. He almost shot his sister in the face. She was running across the projects with a baseball bat, called herself coming to help them go to war. She didn't even know what was actually going on out there that night. Sheed called her a couple of dumb so and sos and told her to go back in the house. They decided to leave, but they knew they had to pay. He went past the house and picked up a few things before he shot out to Egg Harbor City to take care of some business. While there, he must have sniffed five to six grams of coke.

During '88 to the beginning of '89 Sean had experienced all types of drugs. He was wide open, deep into the drug scene. There were times when he did drugs all night long. He made a lot of money, but he also had a bad drug addiction. His habit was so serious that there were times when he would hallucinate. One day, not too long ago his brother asked him if he remembered the time he had the whole house on "point." That was a bad scene. He was gathering golf clubs and baseball bats, in fear, saying someone was in the house. There were times when the paranoia was so extreme that he would sleep with double barrel shot guns.

It was you or him, and he was determined that it would

40

be you. He recalls one night, he almost shot his brother in the face with a flair gun. He was playing around with it, all highed up. He was sniffing, sniff some more, pop some more. This went on for a while, when he cocked it and pulled the trigger, forgetting he had a shell in it. His brother was sleeping, with his head hanging off the side of the bed. The flair shot right past his face waking him. When a flair gun is shot, a ball of fire comes out, goes up in the air and then back down. It burned a hole in the carpet.

There was no real explanation for what he was doing. He started selling drugs to get things, but he had no real explanation as to why he kept selling or why he got so high. He was blind and couldn't see the people he was hurting, the damage he was doing to himself and the disappointment he was causing. There people who thought a lot of him. They knew he could do better, but there was no way anyone could break it down to him. The bottom line was, he didn't care, and that's just how it was. Sadly to say, school was not even an issue during that time. He was enrolled at the Alternative School, but he hardly attended. His mom didn't approve of his friends, and his sisters knew he was deeply involved in the streets. They were aware of his drug involvement and that he carried a gun, however, they didn't know everything. He really tried hard to keep his family away from his street business. His brother wasn't involved in the game at all during that time. He had it going on, a senior in High School, enrolled in the U.S. Navy and the appearance a young man going somewhere. Tony was wearing braces, glasses, had a new love and it seemed as though all focus was on him, and Cat didn't have any of it. His mom had co-signed for him to get a 1980 Volvo, which put him on top of the world.

Sean and his mom had a special relationship. He

felt like there were four people who really loved him, his mother, his grandmother, his aunt Ruby and his girl Tara. They showed unconditional love for him, because no matter what he did they were on his side. They would ball him out quietly behind closed doors, but overall, they stuck up for him. As far as his parents were concerned, there were limitations as to how far they would extend themselves. He had one to implicate me in a situation that he had nothing, whatsoever, to do with. He was passing through the halls at school one day and this cat was all over this chick. The next day the principal called him down to the office and told him that he instigated a fight between them. Fortunately, the chick said he had nothing to do with it.

Have you ever heard the expression, "pressure busts pipes?" Well that saying described Cat's relationship with his dad. They would "just beef" when in the same room with each other. He felt like his dad couldn't stand him, therefore, he wanted him to feel like he couldn't stand him either. One day Sean came home, after being gone for about four days, and he spoke to everybody except for his dad. He was seventeen at the time, and still had a bad attitude problem. He had a couple of drinks earlier, so he knew what happened next, along with his attitude and stubbornness, contributed to their falling out. His dad said, "You are not going to walk in my house and not speak to me." He replied, "Well, I guess it's time for me to go." He turned and walked toward the door, and he stepped in front of him. Sean said, "Excuse me." trying to move around him. His dad said, "I told you, you are not going anywhere, I'm tired of you thinking you can do whatever you want to do." The whole time he had his finger in Sean's face, moving closer and closer. He got a sarcastic look on his face and went to the back of the house. His mom was in the bathroom doing her hair, getting ready for church. He backed all the way to the bathroom door, planting his foot behind him, like he was marking his turf. His dad said, "You ain't going nowhere." Sean had this look of disgust on his face, then he jumped at him, you know, like guys do in the street.

He didn't expect what came next. Boom! His dad punched him in his jaw. He dropped, hit the floor and ran into his bedroom and grabbed the closet door. His pistol was in one of his pockets in the closet. He didn't know what he intended to do with that gun if he had gotten his hands on it, but he did know there was much rage stemming from the two of them. He noticed the window was opened, so he jumped out of the window and bounced. He ran straight to his aunt Ruby's house. She told him he could stay there. They sat up and talked for a long time with aunt Ruby laying down the rules. She said he had to work and go to school if he wanted to stay there. His first instinct was to get a job, and he knew he could get back into the Alternative School. He job searched for a couple of days, when suddenly aunt Ruby told him he had to go back home. "I can't" he told her. "Yes you can," she said. He found out that one of his parents told her that she was wrong forgetting involved and that if she told him he couldn't stay there, he would go back home. He really wasn't mad at her for her decision, but he continued to run the streets. Cat stayed out for days at a time, more than ever. He'd go home, when his dad wasn't there, get some sleep and leave before he got home.

He was running to New York and Philadelphia on a regular basis. His major connections in both spots, had gotten so raw. Major killings and robberies were taking place constantly. He would have to go up five to six stories to cop drugs. Some others would go up, do their business, only to come back down to maybe the second level and get robbed by the partners of those that sold them the drugs in the first place. The drugs were then resold. To his advantage, the joker he was dealing with, provided protection for him from his car to the building and back to his car. The "stick-up boys" knew he was from Jersey. The plan was, he would call twenty minutes to a half hour away, and then he was escorted from his car, searched, tell the man what he wanted and then two armed guards escorted him back to his car.

They had gigantic bags of bricks of cocaine. Between '87 and '88 drug dealers were actually having shootouts with DEA Agents. It was normal to hear of a cop being shot during a shoot out. In all that activity, Cat still couldn't see the danger he was subjecting himself to. He was on a mission to "get that cain." With friends and associates ending up in an early grave or in prison, he never visualized that he could end up the same way.

Things had gotten hot and heavy on the block with some man or woman's son or daughter caught up out there. Bodies were showing up in unexpected places. Things had slowed down a little for him. Behind all the madness, he was trying to slow his life down a little. One day his brother called him to take him to Wildwood for a court appearance. He was there with some cats from Bacharach, and they ended up in a confrontation with three cats from Wildwood. His brother wasn't as wild as he was, although you'd better know what you were doing if you messed with him. He'd fight at the drop of the dime. I told you earlier how they were trained. Tony was known more as a "pretty boy," not a fighter. If you got out of pocket, he'd take you out, check you in a minute. If they had to form as a team, that's the way it had to be. If you came around a corner and saw one of them fighting, you were jumped because that's the way their dad had it. That's the way he was brought up. "If your brother fights, then you fight." There were many who got jumped in Pleasantville and Atlantic City. It's not that they were killers or anything like that, they just handled their business. But overall, Tony was on some layed back thing. When Cat picked him up, they dropped their mom off to work at Prudential first, and then Sean began sniffing coke, all the way to Wildwood. I don't think there was an ounce of fear in him. It was no secret that he liked doing drugs. He left his stash in the car while Tony was in court. One their way home, he can recall Tony asking him why he was always sniffing that stuff. Thinking back one that day, he realized that was one of the "realest" questions he ever asked him. He just told him, "man it ain't nothing." He asked him why he was doing so much, and he told him he wasn't going to sniff too much, and that he knew what he was doing. He was trying to get him off his back. Like I said before, that was his life and he didn't want his family in "his world." Since they grew up fighting so much, this was the first time his brother showed concern for him, or just maybe, staying on the move, he didn't give him a chance. Tony showed him how much he cared in just a few sentences. He said, "I don't like you doing that. I woke up a few times at night and saw you sniffing that stuff, I wanted to say something to you. Can you stop?" He told him, "I don't want to stop, this is how I'm living." Tony looked at him and said, "Then give me some." He said, "nigga, I ain't giving you none of this s***." He asked, "why not? you do it."

He grabbed the twenty to let his brother try it out, however, because he had never indulged in the drug scene before, he almost did the whole bag in one shot. He failed to tell him how to tilt the bag to get the contents all on one side, then he would take a quill and slide it over gradually. Tony started swirling all over the road, he became all emotional and acting like anyone else not used to the stuff. He told Cat that he was afraid he was going to kill someone and end up in jail the rest of his life. Believe me, he knows now, but didn't realize it then, that if he didn't have his mother's and grandmother's prayers, he more than likely would have ended up doing some heavy time or possibly in his grave. Instead of trying to discourage him, Cat began telling him that he had strong connections out in the street and that he needed someone on his team that he could trust. "I need you dog," he told him. He was still telling Sean that how scared he was for him. He remembers seeing a tear roll down his cheek. He didn't know if it was the cocaine or another reason.

Tony was approximately one and a half months from graduating high school and leaving for the military. He proved to be a leader because he had about two or three classmates going in under a buddy plan, which would qualify him to enlist at a higher rank. He asked his girlfriend to marry him, and she said she had to ask her mother, who said no. I'm not saying that was the reason for his failures, but Tony's life began to change from that point on. He got kicked out of school, got his car repossessed, and one year later, he did his first bid in county jail. When he came home, he was on some wildlife s***.

Chapter Three

As fate would have it, one day Cat was visiting relatives, and met a young lady there. He and Tara were going together at the time, but for some reason, he was attracted to her. He saw a deep sadness in her eyes. They started kicking it, and he was really feeling shortie. They stayed in contact with each other, sometimes she would braid his hair. They began seeing each other regularly, and one day she asked him if he had a girl, actually she knew he did, but he said no. Shortie lived with her mother and two brothers in an empty apartment in Absecon when he met her. As they became closer and closer, he didn't pay much attention to what was going on. A family member of his who knew that family, tried to tell him not to get involved with that "family," were the exact words. Of course, he wasn't trying to hear it. They didn't go into details because they knew both of them. He was upset later on in life based on the outcome.

In 1988, they were seeing each other on a regular basis for approximately five to six months. Cat became blinded by drugs, his money wasn't right and he almost moved into the apartment with them. He and shortie were spending a lot of time together, but things had changed. Her brother helped her get a job at Wendy's. Soon after that, he got a job at Wendy's. One day the manager said something slick to him about working there. Cat told him that he could make more money in one day that he makes in one week. He said, "I'll fire you." He told him, "you don't have to, I quit." He didn't realize he was hurting himself.

One day he woke up thinking strongly about the whole situation. Things weren't right. He thought about the fact that he was sleeping on the floor, when they were together, yet he had a bed at home, so he called his mother. He can remember her asking him if he was sure he was ready to come home. She told him that there would be rules that he would have to abide by. The number one rule was that there would be no guns in the house. When his mom picked him up, wouldn't you know it? He had a twenty-five automatic in his bag. In his mind he was thinking that he was making a start to get himself back together by going back home with his parents. But he really wasn't because he went back to breaking the rules from the door. As he unpacked his bag, he felt bad because he lied about the gun. He had all intentions of doing the right thing. His mom gave him "the speech" on how she convinced his dad to let him come back home. He and his dad spoke, but they didn't have much conversation for each other.

He got a job at Trump Plaza as a Bar Porter. One day he saw an ex-girlfriend in Atlantic City. They hadn't seen each other for a couple of months, and started kicking it, until one day she just left, moved to Philadelphia. One day before she left, she asked to hold some of his jewelry, and of course he was mad because she didn't return his jewelry before she left town. He found out later that her mother was staying with one of her friends and she had to move. Shortie went to Philadelphia to stay with her sister. About four months later she moved back and was four or five months pregnant. Naturally Sean started counting months back. One day he asked her, "What's up?" she said, "You don't have to worry about it." He asked her if she was going to kill the baby. She said,

"You don't want me." He wanted to know if the baby was his. He took her for an ultrasound and the doctor said she was having twins and that she was either nineteen and twenty or twenty and twenty-one weeks pregnant. He really couldn't understand how that could be, so he questioned the physician who read the ultrasound. He had never heard of twins being conceived one week apart. He pulled him aside and said, "if you're trying to figure out if you're the father, I don't have anything to do with that, I'm just telling you how many weeks pregnant she is." Cat's mother was a twin. She lost her sister at the age of thirty-eight years old as a result of a car accident. They heard the chances of twins usually skip a generation and one of the children of a twin stands a good chance of having twins. His whole world was about to turn upside down.

Twins, it was a happy thought, but something was wrong. He recalls at the age of sixteen, an old girlfriend had two miscarriages. He didn't know if she was too young or if she just wasn't strong enough. The thought even occurred that something could possibly be wrong with him. So now, here he is with this girl having twins, and he always wanted a baby. Tupac wanted a baby to see part of him that wasn't hated. Powerful lyrics can be found in a song. Cat always felt that the odds were against him, that he was an underdog. That made him fight even harder. Sean's father looked for his brother to be the dominant one, therefore Sean hated for people to look at him as the smallest one. He played harder on the football field for that reason. Cats on the streets hated him because they thought he couldn't get the job done because he was "too small." He always had to work harder to prove himself, however, he proved to be a "true champion, not an underdog."

He was smart enough to take shorts, when the other

49

fella had to have straight paper. As long as there was money to be made, he was out there to make that profit. Different ones wondered why he was stacked up with loot and why everybody was coming to see him.

There were a couple of cats out there at the time who were jealous of his moves, and I'm sure there were some other issues. Jealousy has always been a problem with black people. Cat tried not to deal with competition, just tried to be the best that he could be. He could care less what the other joker got, he did what worked for him.

One day on his way home from work, Cat had another confrontation with the law. It's funny how when you're young, you hardly ever give thought to what you're involved with and how it will affect your future. Like I said, he had a job at Trump Plaza, which at the time, the casinos had a lot more to offer than most jobs in the area. He could eat three meals, two cold and one hot meal. So it really appeared as though if you worked in the casino industry, you were getting a lot. He made decent money along with tips, and a nice benefit package. I made anywhere from three hundred to four hundred fifty dollars a week plus his tips, which was pretty good money compared to what he made in the fast food restaurants. It wasn't the thousand dollars he was accustomed to making. For some reason he always seemed to have a problem getting to work on time. He got away with it working at the fast food restaurants, but working in the casinos, you got written up for being late five minutes. He hadn't been there long and had sixteen points, so kind of knew he wouldn't be there long. Now, even though he was straight during this time, he had a couple of his co-workers to ask him if he knew where they could get some blow. He was a recovering drug dealer, but he found out he wasn't fully recovered. He served them, and before he knew it, he had ten to fifteen regular customers there on his job. Cat was screwing up on a different level.

They started changing his shifts around, from swing shift to graveyard and back, so one day he overslept. To his surprise, when he called in he was told to come in, and that they were glad to know he was coming in. So he was walking up the street on his way to catch the bus, when he ran into this cat who lived on the south side and who always tried to be accepted. He did whatever to get in the "in crowd." Cat asked him for a ride. Just as they approached the toll booth, they saw four state troopers. They later found out that there was some threat to blow up one of the casinos.

Naturally, they were pulled over, four black men, I guess looked suspicious. The driver had a wave scarf on his head, which Cat had snatched off and told him to "just drive." So he jumped out of the car when they were pulled over and started making conversation with one of the officers, which made him look guilty of something. He said, "Nice day, hugh officer." They ran his papers, then they came over to the car and said that he gave them permission to search the car. He knew by law it was illegal for the officers to pat them down. They can pat you down if there is a routine search, to make sure you are not armed, but they cannot go into your personal property. There are some officers who don't care and will do all kinds of things that are against the law in order to make an arrest, because the average person is unaware of what is and what is not legal. Cat had a utility knife on him that he used on the job. When the officer asked him what he was doing with it, he told him where he worked told him it was easier for him to open boxes. He said, "I understand," however, he felt something soft in his pocket and asked him what it was.

Cat said, "It's not a gun." He said, "What?" He said, "It's not a weapon." He then told him to take it out of his pocket. He told him he didn't have to. He said, "listen my man, you just patted me down, I don't have a weapon, I gave you the box cutter, showed you my ID where I work, I don't have a weapon so I don't have to empty my pockets." One of his partners heard the conversation and came over to ask what the problem was. Cat repeated to him all that he had said to the other officer, and also told him, "I know the law." During all this conversing back and forth, he glanced over toward a nearby motel across the marshes, contemplating to make a run for it. He seemed to have read his mind and said, "Don't even think about it. I will shoot you." That cancelled that out right away.

The officer looked at him, and then he pulled him to the back of the car and told him that his partner gets a little hot headed sometime. He then asked, "What you got?" A little weed, coke? We can take care of that." He looked him dead in the eyes and said, "I have some coke." He asked, "a little or a lot?" he told him a little bit. He said, "We can take care of that. Give it here." Cat pulled the coke out of his pocket, and he said, "Put your hands on top of the car, you're under arrest. "They ran a check on him and found out that Buena had a Bench Warrant out on him for $5000.00. His so called straight life was headed downhill once again.

In 1987, Cat was riding through Buena with his brother, who had a problem falling asleep behind the wheel. He had crashed a few cars up as a result. So on this particular day he was falling asleep and Sean yelled, "yo." He told Cat he had to drive. He was all highed up and had no driver's license. His man Boo was in the back seat. He whipped the car out going fifty-five in a thirty-five mile an hour vicinity. They had a radar detector but a cop coming from the opposite direction made a U turn and came after them. He followed them a mile or so before turning the lights on to stop them. He said, "I caught you speeding down the road a little bit." He asked for license, insurance and registration. Cat asked Tony, who was on the front seat, for the insurance card and registration. He gave them to him, and the officer repeated to Sean that he needed his driver's license. Sean turned and asked Tony for his license, that's how messed up he was. He said, "no, I need to see "your" license. He told him he didn't have one. Tony's license was suspended and Boo didn't have his with him. The officer gave him a ticket and took them to the station to make a call for someone to come get them. He pulled them out of the car one by one searching and patting them down. He had a quarter of an ounce of weed on him that he had stuck down his drawers. His jacket was thick enough, but if he got caught every time he was "unlawful," I can't imagine how far in life he'd be now. One way or another, those troopers would have had him, because he knew they would have run his name and the Buena warrant would have surfaced. He ended up in the county jail about a week, missing work, so he got fired.

There are certain things he learned as a result of his unfortunate circumstances. First of all, you have to know when to shut your mouth or bite your tongue. A number of police officers have an attitude and a gun, someone gave them authority (over you). Take for instance Sean's cousin, Rodney King and a number of others, who try to speak their mind, and they end up running their mouth at the wrong time, and saying the wrong thing. We are taught to speak out minds, but have to learn control. There's a time to speak, and a time to just be cool.

When he came home, the only thing Cat had was his pistol. He talked to one of his boys, and told him how he had gotten jammed up. He was one of his connections. He asked him what he was going to do. He let him know he didn't want to go back out on the block. He told him he was already cased up and wasn't trying to get another one. He said, "With twins coming, you gotta do something."

Sean's mom was really disappointed. She had given him another chance by letting him come back in the home. She just looked at him as if to ask, why are you doing this? "What's the problem son? talk to me" she said to him. He didn't know how to tell her what was going on in his life, and frankly speaking, he didn't want to tell her. He didn't want to break her heart. When things got real bad like I said earlier, his mom, grandmother, his aunt ruby and later Tara, were the four people he felt really cared. They never turned their backs on him. His mother knew he was treated differently, and everyone knew he was the outcast in the family. But He had messed up and his mom told him there was no way she could explain this to his dad for him to allow Sean to return home. Tears were swelled up in her eyes as she told him.

Even though shortie was pregnant with the twins, Tara and Sean were still going together. He had no money, no job and his mom was upset with him. His life was really in a state of confusion, going with one girl, and trying to take care of another girl pregnant. He didn't want it to be said that "he didn't take care of his kids while she was pregnant." You know the routine an absent father goes through. He felt as though, if she's pregnant with his baby, or should I say babies, he should be there to help. Shortie's mom paid a weeks rent in a local motel for her one day when she got her income tax check. She and her mom knew Sean couldn't go back home, so she asked him to stay there with her because she didn't want her there alone. A partner of his worked at Beefsteak Charlie's and was able to hook him up with a job there also.

One day in January or February of 1989, Tara asked Sean if there was something he had to talk to her about. He said no, she asked, "Are you sure?" He said, "no." Then she just came out with it. "Sean, do you have some girl pregnant?"

He turned, and looked at her and said, "I don't know." She asked, "Did you sleep with her?" He told her he did but he wasn't sure if the baby was his or not. She started crying. He felt real bad because it hurt him to hurt Tara, especially like this. He explained to her that he couldn't sit back and not help shortie if the baby was his, and assured her that he would get a blood test.

Tara then said, "I don't care about the girl, and I don't care about the baby, you better not leave me." He knew she was a good girl. She never hung out in the streets, she didn't get high and she was a school girl, determined to get her education. She stuck by him since he was in Sandy Hook Youth Facility. Now the other girl, and the one he was messing with before her, did hang out in the streets. They did "gangster stuff. You know, ran the streets, just hung out with the boys.

In a couple of months, Tara's junior prom was coming up. Her mother paid for everything, all Cat had to do was show up. He was working at Beefsteak Charlie's and staying with his baby's mama, therefore, he ended up not going to the prom. He was young, confused and his life was out of control, and it was all his fault. He didn't know why he did some of the things he did. He observed one thing concerning his actions. As long as he was not dealing drugs, he didn't get high. But as soon as he got involved again, straight off the top, he took a sixteenth or a gram for his own personal use. It was a deep situation, and something he had to deal with mentally. As long as there were no drugs in his possession, he had control of himself. In his earlier years, He could sniff a sixteenth with two or three other cats. During this time he could do a gram all by himself. He new he had to get himself together.

One of his cousins had an apartment in Pleasantville with his girl and their kid, and also expecting another baby. His brother and his girlfriend rented a room from him. One day they had a fight and she moved out. Then his brother moved out, So he asked his cousin if they could rent a room from him because the motel rent was killing him financially. They were only there about three weeks before shortie went into labor. Cat was at the hospital the whole time, through all the screaming, crying, and name calling. This was the first time he had ever seen anything like that. It tripped him right out, going through the dilation process, everything! She was in labor for quite some time, and it was a wild scene for a cat to go through, but he sat right there. So finally the baby's are here.

Cat went down to the nursery and just sat there, maybe twenty minutes to a half hour, looking at these twins, one of them light skinned and the other dark skinned. Now Sean's light skinned, bright light, and the babies' mama may be lighter than he is. It wouldn't take a rocket scientist to figure out that if a baby is born dark skinned, he's going to become even darker. He asked shortie why she doing this to him. Tears began to roll down her face. Then her mother started yelling, "she just got finished having those babies" and so on and so on. He yelled back, "shut up, you don't have anything to do with this." The baby's mama then began crying and swore on her father that they were his kids. When she did that, he believed her. He didn't believe in swearing on anything, and for her to swear on her dead father, who she was very close to, made him believe her. Shortie's father had died when she was a little girl. She told him that they had a real close special relationship with each other. So he signed the birth papers with no problem, even though he did tell her that he better not find out that they weren't his kids.

Shortie and the twins stayed in the hospital for a couple of days. When Cat returned the following day to see them and was getting ready to leave, shortie was trying to keep him there. He kept telling her that he'll be back. (Tara must have called and told her she was on her way there) She said, "Don't leave yet." He left anyway and just as he was stepping off the elevator, Tara and her cousin Tammy were getting on. He asked her, "What are you doing here?" She said, "I came to see a friend," he said, "she ain't your friend and reminded her that he was going to get a blood test to make sure they were his. She still persisted, so he told her to just go on, but don't think for one minute she was a friend of hers. Her cousin butted in, "Sean you can't do that." He told her and her mom to mind their business. She said, "She is my business." Sean told her to go ahead up there and left to go to the store.

When he came back, everybody had left except him and Tara, "I told you to leave" She said, "I want to get this straightened out." He told her that he couldn't get a blood test until the babies are six months old. The two of them were sitting there with this, "choose thing, who do you want to be with, me or her?" Because Tara came up there after he had told her not to, he told her he wanted to be with shortie.

Tara said, "Sean, you're going to sit here and tell me that you don't love me?" he answered, "no, I don't love you." She was smiling and said, "You're lying, you know you love me, but that's alright." Then she got up and left. Sean called her later and asked her why she came down there and what was she trying to prove by coming down there. He said, "All you did was caused more problems, and I can't walk away from my responsibilities."

For seven and a half months, he played the daddy role with the pampers, milk, cloths, and cribs. He got some he from his family. It's hard enough paying for one, and when you have two, that's double responsibility. One day shortie applied for welfare. He knew the caseworker. He used to play football with her son. Since he signed his name on the birth papers, they pulled him in for child support. They wanted him to pay. When the caseworker asked shortie if she had a problem with parental testing, she said no. She said, "You're being awfully calm about this. Most girls come through here act up with a lot of confusion." She told them that the results would take six to eight weeks to come back.

They all were still at the apartment, with mad drama going on. His cousin had a fight with his girl and left her. This was the same one that was in the Harbor Fields with him. One day he came by and just broke a window. Sean asked him, "What did you do that for?" He said, "I'll do whatever I want, this is my apartment." Cat didn't know that he went to the landlord and told him he didn't live there anymore and that somebody broke into the apartment and moved in. The landlord was Greek and spoke broken English. When he came by Sean explained how he was his cousin and that was his girl friend and kid and she's expecting a baby. Cat said since he said he moved out, does that mean this apartment is for rent? He asked Sean if he had a month and a half security. He told him he could get it, so he gave him 48 hours to get the money up.

He needed six hundred forty eight dollars. He tried to barrow from a couple of people. He was scared to hustle, so he decided to pawn his jewelry. The landlord asked him whose house he wanted to put the lease in? Since he had to do about six months in the county, he put it in shortie's name. Her family knew the system and all the ins and outs on how to get help for utilities and other things. Cat got knocked off and got a sentence of forty-five days in the county. When he came home, her whole family had moved in. He knew her mom would be there to help out with the kids and at the time save money to get her own place. One day he let her know, "either your family goes or I got to go." He couldn't live there with them, so she told her mom they had to leave. Her brother had the nerve to say to her, "How can you tell your mother she has to leave after all she's done for you, because of some nigga?" Cat had to get with him then. He said, "yo man, I'm the one who pawned jewelry to get this apartment, I don't have to explain anything to you, in fact, you can get you coat and meet me at the door. You got to roll right now."

Eventually, they all left. Her mom knew her little secret, so I guess she opted to leave and work on getting close to him before he found out what was going on. But shortie had a real jealousy problem, and I'm sure it's a problem stemming from her past somewhere. He could be gone only five minutes, just around the corner to the store, only to come back to a whole lot of accusations, mainly concerning calling his girlfriend. She'd start fighting him, ripping his cloths, and she was famous for scratching his face up. They had a very bad relationship. On very few occasions, they did have good times together. The worst thing he could do then, so he thought, was to abandon his responsibilities. So he endured it, got another job and eventually started hustling again. He was trying to get ahead, but there were inside obstacles holding him back. It seems as though every time you try to do something right, there are unforeseen obstacles, or vices, right there to try to stop you from doing what you purposed to do. It could be someone in your family, someone close to you or maybe even something within yourself. It's hard to get ahead this way.

While waiting for the results of the blood test for paternity, the eight weeks had come before he knew it. Since he wasn't, at that time, supposed to be living with the babies' mother, his copy of the test was being sent to his parent's house. They lived in a duplex.

So at times they wouldn't get mail for up to four days, because there mail was accidently placed in the front mail box. One day Sean said, "Yo, the blood test should be here by now, did you hear anything yet?" She answered, "No." The babies needed pampers and milk, so he told her he'd be right back, he was going to the store. He stopped at the phone booth across the street to call his mom, since it was a couple of days since he had seen or talked to her.

When his mom answered the phone and heard his voice, she said, "boy, you have mail here from the superior court, did you get in trouble and didn't tell me about it?" He told her no and that he hadn't been anywhere. She asked, "Are you sure?" He said no and told her to open it up and read it to him. When she started reading it, she said it must be the blood test because she had never seen any papers like those before. Sean became inquisitive and asked what did it say. She told wait a minute and she kept reading and then she asked him where he was at. When he told her, she told him she wanted him to come to the house before he went back across the street. Right then and there, he knew what it said. He went straight to the front mail box, snatched up the mail, putting the blood test results on the top of the stack, and when she answered the door, he shoved the mail at her pregnant chest; You see, she was now five months pregnant with his baby. He told her to read the one on the top first and that he would be right back. Even though, he had just found out they were not his babies, he still went to buy the pampers and milk.

When he got back, she was sitting on the bed. He asked her what she had to say about it, and she replied, "Boo, I swear to god on my father..."he cut her off before she could finish saying what she had to say. He told her "my grandmother could have taken the that blood test and I would have known if they were my babies or not. Why are you sitting here lying?" She then turned crying, begging him no to leave her, that she loved him. He told her to tell him who the father was. This broad had the nerve to ask him if she told him who the father was, would he stay? He looked at her and said, "You're lucky I don't kill you. All I know is, my man owes me money." He snatched her up a little bit, but wouldn't hurt her, she was carrying his baby that he knew was his. He just bounced, but he knew that obviously, the plan was to make sure she got pregnant, so when he does find out the truth about the twins, he won't leave. However, the plan didn't work, he was out of there.

He left, but he was really hurting, hurting bad. He wasn't worried about embarrassment, he was relieved that he found out the truth before five or six years. In that little bit of time, he was attached to them. The sad thing is, she knew all along who the father was.

Once again, He moved back in with his parents for a minute. It took him a minute to regroup and to get himself together. He still had to deal with Shortie because of his daughter that she was carrying. Reality had set in, so he stopped hustling, got a job at TGI Fridays. With this awakening, he wanted to do the right thing. Sean was trying to figure out what he was going to have for this baby and where would he be in ten years. It was just as scary that he couldn't answer the either question. He began evaluating his life, looking at his past mistakes and concluded that he had to get it together. He was nineteen years old and just beginning to realize just how much trouble he was in. Sean was brought up in the church, made to go as a kid, yet he had no direction for his life. He had no knowledge of how to live outside "street life," and that also was a scary thought.

He realized he had made a big mistake in choosing who he wanted to be with. Tara stuck by him through thick and thin. She made him mad, and he reacted the wrong way, making wrong decisions, such as deciding to stay in the situation he was in, which caused their relationship to go sour. Even when she found out about the pregnancy, her reply was, "I want you to take care of your baby, but you'd better not leave me." Tara was a good woman. Sean met her when he was fourteen years old. He taught her how to kiss, that's how special their relationship was. Cat had never had a good woman; therefore, he didn't know what a good woman was about. So now their relationship was done. I guess he took for granted the fact that since they were together so long and he was her first love, that she would always love him. But he knew it was over. She wouldn't speak to him, nor would she receive his telephone calls. He knew he had messed up, but he didn't realize how much. He saw her on several occasions on the street, and she wouldn't give him the time of day. One day he was riding with his mom and they saw her walking in the rain on her way to her aunt's house. His mom pulled over and stopped the car. She came over and spoke to her but just looked at him. When she offered to take her where she needed to go, of course she declined and said she was ok, and then looked over at Cat and said, "I'd rather walk." That hurt him so bad. His mom told him to let her go, that if it was meant for them to be together, it would happen. She told him that Tara was hurting now and she needed time to heal.

One day Cat went into one of the neighborhood bars and ran into a young lady he had a crush on a few years back, although she wasn't aware of it. He walked in, she was sitting at the bar, turned and asked, "how you doing?" They hung out that night and he gave her his phone number. She wouldn't give him her phone number because she was engaged. She told him she would call him the next day at 4:00. He played himself by waiting for the call until 7:00. She didn't call that day, but the next day he received a call from her. She asked to speak to Sean; He asked "who?" She replied, "Oh you don't know me now huh?" Then he said, "oh yeah, you were supposed to call yesterday." They started kicking it. She asked him if he wanted to go with her to her friend's house, and he said yes. A few days later, he found himself in a relationship with her on the rebound. Sean didn't consider himself a sucker for love, but he was at the time, kind of vulnerable. They then began a seven to eight month relationship.

So once again he's back home with his parents, struggling with a $600 every two week income. By the time he hit them up with rent, buy himself a little something, he had hardly anything left over. He wasn't used to not having "plenty of money." One day his mom asked him to go to church with her in Delaware. She was always asking him to go, and when he said yes he would go with her on the following Sunday, he never heard such a loud hallelujah, thank you Jesus before! He said to her, "Mom, I just said yes that I'd go to church with you." She said, "I'm just happy you're finally going with me."

Sunday came and they rolled down to Delaware. He made sure he had his headset on. His mom listened to gospel, end every once in a while, she's look over at him smiling. He knew she was happy. Now, at the time he didn't really understand spiritual matters, even though he was brought up in the church since the age of seven. So when they got to the church, everybody was happy, excited, praising the lord and all. They were going off! He can recall there was a visiting speaker. The pulpit was acknowledged. There were quite a few visiting ministers who gave remarks. During this time, he had the most supernatural experience in his life. Like I explained his experience with cocaine, the feelings he had that day cannot compare. He actually felt his spirit shake on the inside. There was another Minister present, Elder Waltz, who later became Sean's uncle that began to give honor to God, praising him for bringing him through and speaking about the joy of being among the saints, He was expressing how much God had done for him, and then he just stopped in mid-sentence. He said the lord had just spoke to him and told him that there was someone there who needed to surrender their life to the lord tonight! He went to say, "God has spared your life on more than one occasion and you really need to give your life to God today." As he was speaking, he was looking over the audience. Fear gripped Sean's spirit and he knew he was talking to him. He said to himself, "man." He continued, on numerous occasions repeating, "God has spared your life. Were not here to embarrass anyone, but the Holy Spirit will allow me to point you out." He was still looking over the audience, and just as he finished the sentence, their eyes met, and Sean knew he was talking to him. Immediately, the devil jumped on him. If you ever experienced having contact with the devil, you know how he operates. He may put an abrupt thought in your mind or you'll hear a loud voice, which will take your mind off what is going on; or you may be in a calm relaxed state of mind, and something crazy will pop in your head, like someone kicking a door in. The devil operates with confusion, attacking ruthlessly. God speaks to you in a soft voice. You may hear something like, "now you know you're not supposed to be doing that."

So immediately, this abrupt voice speaks, "it's a setup, your mother told them you were coming and they set you up!" Then fear was replaced with anger. He sat there thinking to himself, all the time mad as fire, "I can't believe my mother did this. She told them I was coming and they tried to scare me into coming into the church." By this time, he's not trying to hear anything he's saying. But he continued, "Were not trying to embarrass you, just pray and ask God to guide you." His mind was made up, he didn't want to hear anything. Sean was convinced his mom had set him up to this. After service, elder Waltz walked up to him and asked, "How are you doing young man?" He answered, "I'm alright." He asked him how he enjoyed the service. And he told him it was ok. He said, "good," good we'll be looking forward to seeing you again." He was saying to himself, "don't hold your breath, I won't be coming back," and at the time giving him a look like, yeah, whatever. He was heated! He was furious. His mom didn't know though how he was feeling.

His mom had to speak to some of her sisters in Christ before leaving. That was ok, he just waited. While driving home, after they rode about an hour, Cat snatched his headset off and said, "Mom, did you tell them I was coming down there?" She didn't know how he was feeling, and she had no idea about the encounter he had earlier that day in church. She looked at him and said, "no, why?" He just looked at her, saying to himself, "you don't have to worry about me ever coming down there again."

Later that week, he got paid and decided to buy a quarter ounce and turn it into a quick $200 to $400, to have some extra cash to go out and buy himself a few things. Like any other time, he had to get high. He was sitting around the club, served three people, and all three came back within fifteen to twenty minutes for more. At first he thought there was a problem with his stuff. These cats cooked it up and smoked it. Cat didn't do all that, they were just pinging and drinking a twelve pack. They remarked, "That's some bad stuff there." Sean made his money back real quick. A few minutes later, one of his partners came by and said he had some weed and asked him if he wanted to smoke a couple of woos. Even though he had already sniffed a half gram of coke, he gave him a half gram to cook up. They went over to his house, which was down the street from Cat's parents. They layed three woos with a half gram of coke from front to back. He was still sniffing while he was hooking the woos up. When they started smoking these wooies, after starting on he second one, he put it out. He wasn't feeling right, and his partner must have seen the look on his face. He looked at him and asked, "Sha, you alright?" He said, "No, give me your hand." He then put his hand on his chest. His heart was beating very, very fast and hard. His partner's eyes got big as a half dollar. He said, "yo man, you wanna go to the hospital?" He said, "No, take me to see my mother." He thought he was going to die, and wanted to see his mom's face before he left there. That's how scared he was and how serious this thing had gotten.

The distance from his house to Cat's was the approximate size of a football field. They started walking, and it actually took them about twenty minutes to get there. Between each step, he thought his heart was going to explode. When they got there, his man just left and went back home. He went in, straight to the bathroom and flushed the rest of the coke he had in his pocket, down the toilet. Then he went to his mom and dad's room and began calling his mom, in a whisper. She finally woke up. Looked at the clock, saw it was 3:30 am and asked, "Sean, what's wrong?" He said, "Mom, I did too much coke tonight." She jumped up and said, "Boy, you'd better get down on your knees and ask God to help you right now."

The only thing he could think about at the moment, was only a week earlier, he had the chance to surrender, and now he was scared to death. He knew if he tried to go to the hospital, he would have died on the way, and the autopsy would have shown that he had large amounts of cocaine, marijuana and alcohol in his system. However, on the real side, a "spiritual battle" was taking place over his life between God and the devil.

Chapter Four

Ten years ago, Cat married the true love of his life, Tara. They were struggling at the time with no apartment or car, only each other and Jesus, but that was cool. He was out on bail for armed robbery, which he had no knowledge of whatsoever. He didn't even know it happened until he was charged with it. He was offered a plea bargain, but there was no way on God's green earth, he was going to plead guilty to something he knew he didn't do. Just imagine yourself in his passion, supposedly, positively identified and snatched up, just like that. With all the dirt he knew he did in the past, he just knew he wasn't going to jail for something he knew nothing about. So he decided to go to trial, instead of taking a plea bargain, and went with a public defender, which he found out to be the ultimate mistake.

The first trial was real sloppy. His Pastor met him at the courthouse, which some testimony had already been heard when he got there. They were out on recess, so they decided to go to the waiting area. He pointed out the prosecutor and the Detective who charged Sean, and asked him who they were. Cat identified that the two of them and he proceeded to inform him that he overheard the Prosecutor tell the Detective that his witness's testimony was different from what he (the detective) had told. He said the detective became very upset. Word is bond, the Prosecutor put the Detective back on the witness stand and he matched his witness's testimony.

There would have been inconclusive testimony and they would have lost the Wade hearing, so they decided to break the law, do they could go on with the trial. You see, he was promised over and over by this same detective, that he was going to get him. But never in his wildest dreams did he expect so called, "upstanding law officials," to outright break the law in a court of law to pin this crime on him. They were dirty throughout the whole trial. Sean had to ask himself, "I wonder how many other jokers they did the same thing to?"

In his heart, he really believed if the first jury had to deliberate, the case would have been thrown out. They had sad disgusted looks on their faces, as if to ask, "How can they do this to you?" When they picked the jurors, they had two alternatives. Something happened and they ended up with only twelve. A mistrial was called. They had time to go over everything prior to the second trial, even though there was no physical evidence to tie Sean to the robbery. The description they had of the criminal was a five foot four inch to five foot six inch light skinned black male weighing one hundred thirty one to one hundred forty pounds; wearing dark pants with a yellow ski vest and black hat. At that time Cat was five feet nine inches tall, he wore his hair in a boxed haircut with at least four inches of hair on his head, making him look six feet two inches to six feet three inches tall. He was wearing a triple goose down coat, which made him look every bit of two hundred twenty to two hundred thirty pounds. No way did he fit the description. The robber supposedly dropped some money at the door and left a note at the crime scene and Five O found a yellow vest. Everything was messed up from the door. There were two lady witnesses who told two different stories. One of them testified that she looked through every photo at the police station. She said when she asked for more photos, she was told that she looked through them all. This was fifteen minutes after the robbery. There were no fingerprints of his. There was no evidence, and he has all the transcripts and documents from his trial to prove it. Sadly to say, because of all the mistakes and lack of evidence, he just knew he would not be going to jail. One crucial mistake black men make because they can't afford an attorney, is taking the witness stand to testify in their own defense.

He did it and left it wide open for the prosecutor to bring up everything in his past. Cat had a wicked one, but left it all to live for Christ, even taking a job at Burger King to provide for his family. Your past life will come back and bite you sometime. Another mistake is taking a public Defender to represent you, who is working for the State, and the State against you.

The night he was arrested, he was with one of his partners, but what he didn't know is that he was still hustling drugs. He had told all his acquaintants that he was in church now living a righteous life and was through with the dealings in the streets. So now, here he is with this cat, you may as well say he was putting Cat's freedom in Jeopardy. They walked past the Mobile gas station going to use the pay phone, when a police officer ran down on him. He knew him because he played basketball with his son. He had his Income Tax check, so he used it and some cash he barrowed from his dad to bail himself out of jail.

Those in high places who were determined to destroy his life by sending him to prison for a crime he did not commit, meant it for his harm, but God turned it around for his good. The picture started out real ugly at first. He began to tell himself that he'd be glad when this was all over. They ran into a problem that last day the jury was deliberating. They were deadlocked and couldn't come up with a unanimous decision. The judge told the jury that he felt they weren't deliberated long enough, therefore, he was not going to declare a mistrial. Technically, it's supposed to be all over when the jury says they cannot reach a decision. He told them that he wanted them to go back, Start fresh deliberations and they will come back with a unanimous decision. The judge is not allowed to tell the jurors to come back with a unanimous decision. They have a right to voice their opinion. It's against the law, and also his civil rights were violated.

The jurors went back and one of the jurors, I'll call Mr. X, wrote a note to the judge, the note said, "I want to be released from jury duty. I'm steadfast on my decision and I'm not changing my mind."

The judge called him out and told him he was not going to dismiss him. He said, "I can't do it, it's been a long day so I'm postponing the decision until tomorrow." He then told them again to start fresh deliberations. The next day, Mr. X did not show up. The prosecutor advised the court that Mr. X was in a PTI program. When this happened there definitely should have been a mistrial, but instead they stuck an alternate in, they deliberated and came out with a guilty verdict after twenty minutes. Mr. X was a convicted felon who lied in the very beginning. Cat feels he has been treated unjustly by our legal system.

That morning he had kissed his wife on the forehead and told her this should be the last day. That's how sure he was that there was no way he was going to be found guilty. After two and a half months of marriage, with his wife pregnant with his son Sean Jr., who is now nine years old, Cat was snatched away from them.

Just imagine kissing your new wife of two and a half months on the cheek and telling her that this is the last day of court, and that after today it will all be over. But instead, the true nightmare begins. Never in his wildest dreams could he conceive the idea that he would be convicted of a crime that he had no knowledge of at all, but it happened. He was falsely accused, railroaded, convicted and then sentenced to eighteen years in prison! For the life of him, he could not understand why God would allow this to happen to him, after choosing to change his life and his wicked ways and walk with him.

At first he though to himself, "oh this must be the way God is going to show him who he really is." He even told the cats in the county jail that he served a mighty God and on January 24th, he was going home in Jesus name. They all laughed and told him he was crazy. You couldn't convince him no other way, but that they were going to see a miracle on January 24th.

There were a couple cats in there that he knew from the streets who called themselves preparing him for what should happen legally, for the position they had put him in. They respected him and his faith and what he believed in, but they said to him, "listen Bro, I don't want you going in that courtroom thinking you're going home, cause word is bond, that's just not going to happen." Cat said, "Bro, you don't serve the same God I serve." They just laughed and said, "When they give you twenty years, don't come back here acting crazy."

The day he stood in front of the judge, he wasn't scared at all. He really believed that an act of God was going to take place that day. The judge asked if he had anything to say before he sentenced him, and he said yes he did. He said, "I told you and this court from the very beginning that I was innocent, and I maintain my innocence. For some reason, I don't know what, the jury has convicted me, so the only thing I can do is appeal whatever sentence you give me." Why did he say that! The judge gave him the dirtiest look and said, "considering the aggregating factors outweigh the mitigating factors, (he was looking at Sean's extensive juvenile record) "I hereby sentence you to eighteen years in the custody of the New Jersey State Corrections." When he heard eighteen, all he remembers was a real sick feeling in his stomach and almost passing out. His legs almost gave out from under him. It was unbelievable. It really felt like a bad dream. He turned, looked at his pregnant wife, and all he could say was, "I love you."

While in the County jail, he had a few visits from some church members. They tried to comfort him by saying, "just think of it as if you're going to Bible College. We'll be here for you, whatever you need, just call. We'll put money on your books every week to make sure your wife doesn't have any financial pressures." It sounded good when they first said it, but I don't think they fully understood what they were promising or how much Sean was depending on their word. Don't get me wrong, they were there, but not like they promised.

Now there he is with this very big prison sentence, not only falsely accused, but his first trip to state prison. While he was there, Cat decided since the situation was beyond his control, he had to adapt to the environment without getting caught up in any nonsense. The first thing he did was get his G.E.D., and then he enrolled in school for cosmetology. He also completed a course in upholstery and courses in Behavior Modification One, Two and Three. He received special Honorary Awards as Valedictorian.

Prison is a world of it's own. He was determined to do his time and not let the time "do him." In evaluating his teenage years, he realized he had messed up so bad, so he was determined to learn as much as possible. He learned how to play chess, sometime playing twenty to thirty games a day. He went through many ups and downs and became very lonely at times. Every time he went through those times, someway, somehow, God brought him through. Often he found himself in situations where he was threatened because of his stand for God and speaking the truth. It didn't change him in any way, nor did he change his ways.

One day while sitting in his cell a little stressed out, he heard an old song, entitled, "Be Grateful," that his mother use to play when he was a child. The lyrics are: Be grateful because there is someone who is worse off than you: be grateful, for there is someone who would love to be in your shoes." I can't describe what the words meant to him at that time. Tears rolled down his face as he began to think about his situation and the possibility that "it could be worse." The way the system did him so easily, He knew that there were brothers out there that had similar and worse accusations made against them. He talked to himself and visualized brothers out there who had thirty year sentences for something they did not do, and they should be grateful because there are others who are on death row for something they did not do, and still others who have been executed for something they did not do. That was the mentality that helped him get through his bid in prison.

Later, during his prison term, Cat met a brother who really caught his attention, whose name was Big Larry. Almost everyone who has been through the prison system, knew or heard of him. He shows a lot of inmates how to lift weights and train properly. Cat didn't work out like most jokers did, two or three times a day, five days a week. He found it more important to exercise his mind more than his body. He did do a light workout three times a week, trying to stay In decent shape. He saw Big L out there almost every time he went to the weight pile. O'Boy noticed that Cat usually worked out alone, so one day he told Sean that if he wanted to move up in weight that he would spot him. Sean was like, "alright, cool." One day while working out, Big L said to him, "you know what I noticed about you?" Cat asked, "What's that?" He said, "You don't belong here." He laughed and said, "You're right, I shouldn't be here." He asked him how much time he had left, he told him, "I don't know how much time I'll actually do, but I was sentenced to a flat eighteen years for something I didn't know anything about." Big man looked at him and one tear ran down his face. Cat's like, "oh shoot this big joker just got emotional on me, real quick!" It didn't take him long to get himself together and O'Boy said, "listen youngeon, I believe you, but you're going to be alright. You'll be home soon, but I want to tell you something that I don't talk about too much. I've been locked up for eighteen years for something I didn't do." Sometime later, he found out that Big L's charge was from the same city, same corrupt police officer and court system; and here was another famous writer who would do close to thirty years before having his sentence overturned, because at that time Big L was still fighting his case.

While doing his time Cat ran into a couple of cats who had lost loved ones while incarcerated. He saw one brother "go through it" pretty bad. He really felt some of their pain. You know when something is real, because you feel it in your body, particularly in the stomach; "feel me?"

Cat knew he had a few things to straighten out with his pop. One day he called him and he felt as though that was the most genuine conversation they had ever had. It really broke the ice and was the start of a new relationship between them. They were on the phone for almost three hours that day. Not too long after that, they had a family crisis that they all had to deal with. The way his father handled the situation, showed Cat something about him that he never would have imagined. It caused him to look at him totally different, in a way that he could say, "My dad is a hell of a man!" After the initial ice breaking conversation, their relationship grew into a real friendship, which grew into a strong father and son relationship. Now, I'm not going to sit here and tell you that they agree on everything, or that they don't get upset with one another from time to time, because they do. No two people see things the same way; that's what we call "perception." Somehow they always manage to get through their disagreements, and "that's my man," he says. One thing about the O'Boy, he never left them.

Shortly after all this, he finally made it to the halfway house with a little over three years in. He can remember thinking, "it won't be long now!" Finally, he was able to get a job, so he could send more money home to his wife. She is the one who really held him down through his entire bid. She always made sure he had what he needed, food, cloths and money on his books. His parents and sisters and brother brought him food packages and helped him from time to time, but Tara hung in there through thick and thin. Cats down at prison used to see Sean come back from a visit with mad food, cloths, etc. Some would say, "Man I want a wife like that when I get out there." Cat would say, "There is no more." He promised his wife that when he came home, whatever she wanted, he would give to her, if it was in his power to give. He promised to build her a castle, and he meant it, with everything he is as a man. He was at the halfway house with a childhood friend, his man Arron. They also had another cat named Basheem, who ran with them. The three of them did things that were unreal. Both of them bought cars while in there, and Sean and Tara bought a townhouse. He worked at Wendy's for about two months, couldn't put up with managers trying to play him out because they knew he was incarcerated, so he quit.

He then landed a job in a window factory in Camden. One day he went up to the front desk to get a razor blade to cut something, and this joker at the front desk dropped the razor blade straight down in his hand. Cat turned and looked at him like, "no you didn't!" He must have felt his look because he had a real scary look on his face. He then apologized. Later they got real cool. He knew he was in prison, so he used to ask him questions all the time, like, "what's it like?" He told him, he wouldn't last a week. Sean told him one or two things, if not both, would happen to a cat like him. He said, "What's that?" He said, "You would get raped or extorted, and the cats in there would have you calling home every week for protection money." "Dad, please send the money, these guys said they're going to kill me." Then he started laughing, but he had a shook look on his face and asked him if he was serious. He nodded still laughing. One day the owner really pissed him off; when his man G asked him what was wrong, he just said, "The owner is an ass hole!" He said, "yo man, that's my dad." He didn't know it at the time, he then looked at him and said, "so you know I'm telling the truth." The boss had fired Cat seven times, but since his son was big on him, he was always able to talk him out of it.

After approximately eight months in the halfway house, he had his first parole review. There were two woman who had to decide whether or not he deserved a chance for parole. One of them acted as though she was trying to provoke him to anger, but he remained cool as an ice cube. For a minute, she was asking him questions concerning juvenile charges. She asked, "what were you doing carrying a gun at the age of fourteen?" He said, "I don't know, that was nine to eleven years ago. I can't possibly tell you what was on my mind, but that's over and done with now." She then questioned him about his current charge, and he told her that he didn't do it, so he couldn't tell her much. He became very uncomfortable and was starting to become agitated when she told him that he manipulated the system because he didn't have any prison infractions for her to judge him on. He's like, "oh no, not another injustice." Immediately, the other woman changed the interview towards his support system. She told him that he had a very good one and that she thought if he stayed with it, she knew he could make it on parole. The first woman then jumped back into the interview and asked, "How can you go through all the prison time you've gone through without getting into any trouble at all?" He told her, "God is on my side, I mind my business, educate myself and stay away from trouble." They asked him to step out of the room for a minute. About five minutes later, they called him back into the room and told him that they decided to give him a "second chance." Cat was given a release date for January 16, 1996. He told them thank you and assured them that he would make it.

Even though his date was three months away, he was very happy, because based on the way the interview started out, things just didn't look good for him. However, life became very frustrating, knowing he was given a release date so far, yet so close. Life in a halfway house can be upsetting, because anything can happen to deter your release. There's quite a bit of jealousy among the brothers when they learn of someone about to be released. Obstacles came his way, but he was determined he was going to make it home. He knew he had to develop a plan to put his goals into action. There's one thing he learned from all his experiences, everything happens for a reason.

Before his release, he evaluated his life up to that

point. Even though they did him dirty in the court room, he had to pay for all the dirt he thought he had gotten away with from the past. Trust me when I tell you that he had a lot of blood on his hands! He messed up his life as a juvenile, including his education, but one thing he realized was that everybody makes mistakes. The great king David in the Old Testament Scriptures made mistakes, and some of the presidents of the United States made mistakes. But there's one thing he said he would not do; he will never keep looking behind him, because if he does, he will never see what's in front of him. During his second time around, he would continually dedicate his life to do the very best he could do, and pursue whatever dreams he has.

Chapter Five

January16, 1996, Cat was released from the halfway house, in which he had received the date in October of 1995. Before he came home, he tried to prepare himself because he knew there were certain things he would need. He didn't want to have to depend on the old crew he used to hang with. He wasn't looking for anything from anyone in the streets. Number one, he didn't want any strings attached, if he would have accepted any handouts. Number two, he didn't want to set himself up for failures, in the event he was promised help and it didn't come through for some reason or another. Nine times out of ten, this is what usually happens. So Cat made sure he had all his cloths. He had about seven pair of sneakers, four or five pair of shoes, a couple double breasted suits and some sweat suits. He and his wife were fortunate to be able to purchase a townhouse while he was still away, so he had his own place to come home to. It kind of surprised him when his pastor came to pick him up. Several promises weren't fulfilled, which hurt him. He found out first hand that one of the worse things that can happen to a person locked behind bars, is to receive certain promises and they aren't kept.

All you have is a person's word, and if he/she neglects to come through for you, that's a very hurting feeling. Some people will promise what they'll do weekly, monthly or be there to see you at a specific time, and if they go back on their word, it can really crush you. That's the reason why I never give definite promises. I always say I'll do what I can and when I can. It really hurts when it comes through the church. Sean did have some very special people to come visit him who didn't even know him at the time. Bishop Berry and his wife came, Pastor Bordley, Brother Merion, Cat's cousin Shonda, Minister Zeke, Burnside; these people were all instrumental in keeping his faith going when he felt down. They helped to look a brother out.

He tried not to focus on disappointments. Cat had a lot of plans he needed to carry out. The first thing he did when he got out of the halfway house was to buy a dozen roses and take them to his wife at work. Then he purchased two more dozen and placed them from the doorsteps to their bedroom.

He started working right away, cutting hair at his aunt's salon in Atlantic City. The area wasn't that popular for an ethnic cliental, located in the Spanish and Oriental section of the city. This was his first time working on the streets as a barber. Tara was very upset about it and told him one day that he had to get a job somewhere else. He wanted to hang in there with his aunt, but he only lasted there three or four days. He told his aunt that he had to get another spot for walk-ins. She understood and told him that he could always come back after he built his cliental. She told him that the door would always be open; and that was cool.

He went to this brother's shop, which was in Atlantic City also. The gentleman he went to see asked him if he had his license, and he told him no he didn't. So he asked Cat if he wanted his license, and he told him he did. He told Sean to come with him. They went to go get his truck and he told Sean he was taking him to Pleasantville to enroll him in school to obtain his barber license. Because of the conversation between the two of them on the way to Pleasantville, Sean knew they wouldn't get along. His religious views were totally different than what they were before he left prison. Cat strongly believed in what he had studied, therefore, he wanted documentation whenever someone came up with something that sounded like the contrary. My man was singing a different song for whatever reason. Something had turned Cat off. The old man said he was starting a new Bible study and that his barbers were going to be subject to his teachings, and that whoever didn't come to Bible study classes, couldn't cut hair in his shop. Right then and there he knew he wouldn't be working in his shop. He took Cat to the school and he got plugged right up. He was set up right away for an interview to enroll in classes.

Another sister he knew had a shop with two barbers, but they didn't have a license. She wanted to hire him, but she couldn't take a chance on another unlicensed barber. Even though he was in the process of obtaining his license, her response was, that's what they all say." She told him it was nothing personal, and he understood her position. So he went to a shop where he had a promise of employment. This cat who used to cut his hair before he went to prison, told his sister when he heard he was cutting hair, that he had a job for him when he came home. Cat knew him for a long time, and they were always cool, but it took a minute for them to see eye to eye on the money situation. He wanted him to pay $35.00 per day to rent a chair from him, and when he broke it down to him that it averaged out to $840.00 per month, and that was too much, he still insisted. Cat let him know that he wasn't going to let him take advantage of him. He had toys, a van, cars, and a motorcycle, and he wanted toys too. He told him, "You're not going to tell me how to run my shop." He told him he wasn't trying to tell him what to do, he just wasn't going to pay him $210 per week to rent a chair. He was starting school in February, so they agreed that since his classes were from 9:00 to 2:30, he would work from 2:30 to 7:00 and pay him $20.00 on week days and $35.00 on Saturdays. He still had a problem with that because he would be there only part of a working day. On the other hand, he knew he wouldn't be there for long. O'Boy didn't know how much Cat was making, and he didn't tell him. He said that he would work with him until he built up a cliental. He expected a little more from him, since he knew what it was like coming home from prison, trying to get on your feet. But all he cared about was getting that money, not caring where or how you lived, just as long as he maintained his lifestyle.

While he was in prison, Cat had heard about how he had opened a shop and how good he was doing. He was the Man. Word was ringing down in prison of how he had this one and that one and how his shop stayed packed. But when he came home, he was the only one in there. He had lost all his barbers. It seemed odd but, he never questioned it. His business was booming from the first day. He was doing so good one day his wife said, "I can quit my job now." He said, "no you can't either. We have a five year plan we're trying to accomplish." When he first came home, they sat down and worked out a plan for him to get his license, work extra hard and either sell the townhouse or use it for income property, and buy the home they really want. Now she was ready to mess up the plan by quitting her job after he was home only less than a month. He told her he understood she worked while he was away, but that they had to do this together. There was no way he could handle all their expenses. He told her that he wouldn't be making $1200 all the time. They had purchased a little ford escort while he was away, but told her when he got home and they got on their feet, she could get any car she wanted. Of course he was eying a beemer at the time. Their car payment was only $160 a month, so he felt they could swing that along with their other expenses. When it came time to trade the escort in, she decided she wanted a Honda Odyssey. When he didn't show an interest, her response was, "you said I could get any car I wanted." Three weeks later, she had an argument with her best friend and walked off her job.

Cat had anticipated having a little bit of a problem adjusting when he came home, but this was a lot of pressure. He didn't want to crowd in on her and he didn't want her crowding him. He also knew what the Word of God said concerning the man being the head of the household. But his wife had a problem submitting to that. She was the head in his absence, but she still wanted to play the role as head. He's not the type of guy to let anybody run over him, and definitely not a woman. He was down that road as a youth. Coming up he had a woman to try to deceive, manipulate and run over him. It wasn't going to work then and it sure wasn't going to work now. He wasn't going to be told what time he had to be in the house, where he could go and who he could be friends with. That was out of the question. They bumped heads on little things like that. She dramatized things a lot more than they were at times; you know, watching too many soap operas. He would get off work 7:30, sometimes 8:00 at night, and stop past his mother's house. He'd call himself doing the right thing by calling to let her know he'd be home in a little while. She would say something like, "What do you mean over your mother's house? weren't you just over there last night? What are you doing over there again?" He couldn't get with that, not where his mother was concerned.

He started getting a little depressed with school, started loosing interest. But he didn't want to be like the other barbers. He wanted to finish and get his credentials, you know, be legal. Some of those jokers would run out the back of the sop when State Board would show up. He decided to stick it out and finish. It was a rough transition adjusting from the four year prison life to the time spent in the halfway house, and then coming home to his family. He had in his mind that he had to stay focused and do the right thing. He love's a challenge, and that's what he had in front of him. He knew he could do it and he was determined he was going to do it. The one thing he had a time relating to while in beauty school was doing women's hair. He didn't see the sense in all that training, just to get his barbering license.

Cat was struggling everyday, late for school all the time. One day he went around to the shop on his lunch break to heat up his lunch and three guys came up wanting their hair cut. He told them he was on his lunch break, and they told him they had to get out of there. He knew that was a nice tip, so he cut all three in forty-five minutes, and cleaned up his area, skipping lunch. That was a quick $45. The owner came up and told him he had to see him. He said ok. He started in a gruff voice, real stern, "what time do you come to work?" He said, "What?" He repeated the question. Cat said, "yo man, I don't have to report to you." He went on, "what was our agreement? Sean, you aren't due to work until 2:30. You come around here on your lunch break cutting hair, so you gotta pay the shop half the money you made." His blood pressure shot up and he said, "nigga, I'm not paying you s*** and you don't have to worry about me working in your shop." He packed his stuff up and went to leave the shop. My man tried to block him and said, "how you just gonna up and leave? You're wrong Sean." He didn't speak to

Cat for three months or more, but he found out that he couldn't run him. He then went around to the school, packed his things up there and told the instructor that he didn't want to be there any more. He talked to his dad and told him what just happened. He said, "He's not a good businessman and I can't operate like that." His dad said, "Son, you never leave a job unless you have one to go to." But he was able to get another spot right away. He went to another shop and there was an empty chair waiting for him. The owner wasn't there at the time, but one of the barbers told him to go on and set up. But Cat didn't do business like that. The proprietor gave him a spot when she got in. She said, "oh sure baby, you come on over here."

There was another struggle in his life, being able to spend time with his daughters. The four years he was away, I believed he only saw his daughters three or four times. He really felt that it was necessary for girls to have a relationship with their fathers. If they don't, they'll seek love in other places, and nine times out of ten, it won't be genuine. He's seen a lot of damage that can be done first hand. So he really looked forward to seeing them, every chance he got. For whatever reason, their mother wanted to make it difficult for him to see them on a constant basis. The first time he picked them up, they went shopping for cloths and other things. Tara was with them. When he took them home, there was a problem. It seemed as though the girl's mother felt he was trying to turn them against her or something. Whatever was going on with her, she was trying to keep them out of his life. The next week when he went by to pick them up, she told him that she didn't know what he had done to them, but for some reason they didn't want to go with him. Cat knew right then that she had poisoned their minds against him. He had never mistreated either one of his children, nor had he ever slapped or spanked them. She had them trained too as to what to say and do. She said, "Go on take them." When he said, "come on girls let's go," They started screaming and crying, saying no mommy, don't leave us, we don't want to go."

He told her he didn't know what kind of game she was playing, but he had a court order for visitation. It floored him. He couldn't believe she could stoop this low to try to keep him away from his daughters. He told her that she didn't know what she was doing, playing the types of mind games she was playing with the girls at such a young age. "Yeah, whatever," was her reply. She and Sean's wife Tara had all types of verbal confrontations. One day she tried to spit in Tara's face. Tara in return, put the van in reverse and tried to run her over. Cat yelled, "Hey, my kids are back there." The bickering went on for awhile, but Sean was determined to fight to see his children. His mother advised him to leave it alone for a little while, and eventually, they would come around when they were ready. He didn't think that was right. You have deadbeat dads out there not doing anything for their children, and here he was paying child support and still trying to have a relationship with them. Everything seemed to have been backwards. He still wanted to fight, but there was so much tension and drama behind it. The Child Support Office told him to contact the Local Police Department. They told him it was nothing they could do. He tried to get their shots, Dental and medical records from her. All he was trying to do was make sure they were getting the proper medical treatment. She told him she wasn't giving him anything. So he contacted Child support and told them he wanted proof that they were receiving proper medical treatment. They told him the only way was if he went through DYFS and they would have to order an investigation. So that's the route he had to take, and the outcome was a visit from her two uncles.

One of them threatened him, indirectly, which surprised him because he knew him very well. At one time Sean was the only one visiting him down in prison. His family wouldn't even visit him. At the age of sixteen, there Cat was looking him out. Furthermore, he had trained Cat in the streets, brought him up. They used to be cool, Sean knew his moves and knew how he got down. What he didn't expect was for what transpired next. He was standing in front of the shop one day, talking to one of his boys, when he spotted him and his brother coming up the street. They were big cats 6'2" and 6'3". They just walked up to him, put him in a "still", hit him in the jaw and stabbed him in the leg twice. In his wildest dreams, he would never expect him to cross him like that. He had even heard he argued with his niece on more than one occasion about allowing him to see his daughters. A couple cats were standing around on the street, they became real mad when they saw what happened. There was nothing they could do, it wasn't their problem, it was his. He went into the shop, called his wife and told her he was going to the hospital, then he called two of his peoples. He made a trip to A.C. to see one of his people about getting a gun. He said, "man, my niece needs you out here, she don't need you in jail. Just talk to the brother and tell him it's none of his business, it's all about your children." (of course the devil popped his head up, putting thoughts in his head.) Once reasoning came he was able to tell himself, "don't go there, solve this problem another way."

When his partners got in town, there were two from North Jersey and one from New York. They wanted to handle the situation in a way that wasn't cool. His wife begged him not to deal with it on that level. Realistically speaking, if he had allowed them to do what they wanted to do to her, how could he look in his daughter's faces, knowing he had something done to their mother. His pastor convinced him to sign a complaint. He didn't feel right talking to the police after what they had done to him. It was a dead issue as far as him going to court and all that. He wasn't down like that. Even though he was in a spiritual battle with satan, he was glad he was walking with Christ at the time, or it's hard to tell what condition he would have ended up in. Most likely, he would not have been around to tell of it. He had been walking with Jesus five years now, all through his prison bid. He had been in the "belly of the beast," being visited by all types of demonic spirits surrounding him, yet he held onto proclaiming the name of Jesus.

So now that he changed his place of employment, he had to build cliental all over again. He had a decent amount across the street, but those jokers wouldn't inform his customers where he was at. He started running into his customers in the street and was asked why he stopped cutting hair. He told them he was still barbering, and that's when he was told they didn't know where he was. "That's messed up,"one of Cat's partners said. "Do they know where you are?" He asked. Cat told him they did. He knew that was part of the game. He had learned from his man Mark some time earlier, a good man. When he first started cutting, a customer had come into the shop and asked for Jason. Mark responded, "Jason works around the corner." One of the other barbers got mad because he did that. Mark said, "you never try to steal customers. It's like taking food out of someone's mouth." Stealing customers was never part of Cat's game.

It was kind of rough getting started all over again. He had to get his driver's license straight. He never had a license, just a permit, but that had gotten suspended. He had to pay $1700 to become legal, just from fines from the past. His man Basheem came down to help him get through his tests. He bought a little hoopty to get around in. They still had the escort, so one of his cousins was interested in buying it. But his credit prevented him from getting financed. So now he's about to learn another valuable lesson. They let him take over the payments, in which he only had the car a month before it was totaled. Fortunately, the accident wasn't his fault. Someone had run a stop sign, however, they had to pay about six or seven hundred dollars in car payments before everything was settled. The other good thing was that no one was hurt. He had a couple people in the car with him, which it was understood that there were to be no passengers. Some time earlier, he had asked a friend of his to co-sign for him to get a car, and he said no. Cat said, "I thought you were my friend." He said suppose you go out and crashed my car, then I don't have transportation." At the time, he didn't understand. Life is funny, like a revolving door. Sometime we have to go through things before we can relate to something from the past.

Cat had a few hoopties, a trait he inherited from his grandfather, "jockie Joe," They called him. Sean had an '85 Renault Alliance and an '87 Chevy Celebrity Euro Sport, but he wanted a new car. He felt he was taking care of his family; he worked hard, but his past once again caught up to him. He had made some other bad decisions with credit cards. His daughter's mother had purchased various items from Annie Sez and JC Penny, and he went to jail with these outstanding bills, which were never paid. So his credit was messed up and he needed a co-signer. He asked his wife for her assistance, to his surprise, she answered, "you've been home ten months and think you deserve a new car?" Once again, his blood pressure shot up. He couldn't believe what he was hearing. He had come home and right away began paying for a new van for her.

He went to a dealership where on of his friends was a salesman. He picked out a '93 Cougar. He told Cat he could get him financing, but the interest rate would be high without a co-signer. When he told his wife he was going to get the car, she said she wanted to see the car, so he took her with him. Now, she didn't know the salesman was a friend of his, that they grew up together. He couldn't believe what he was hearing from his wife. She tried to mess up Sean's deal and embarrass him in front of his friend. She said, "I don't know who he thinks is going to give him a car. He can't even pay his bills on time." His man turned around and looked at him. He said, "I'll talk to you later." I guess by the look on Cat's face, he could tell he was burning, he was vexed. He took her home, on the way she said, "I suffered for four years, riding buses, driving cars that broke down on the road, you don't deserve to drive a new car." He said to her, "I was in a cage, in a cell with brick walls and steel doors for four years."

He went back alone, and got his car. The interest rate was 22% as opposed to 10 or 11% if she would have worked with him. But she thought he wasn't deserving. They had a real problem within the home. Cat was trying to keep a balance. He went to school, work, Bible study and Church on Sunday. Most of the time, he didn't get home until eight o'clock, and sometimes nine o'clock at night. One day, when he stopped to see his mother, his wife asked, "Where was your mother when you were in prison and I came to see you every Sunday and took care of you?" That was his mother, and it hurt. I'm sure, in fact, I know she would never want anything said like that about her mother.

He was also getting pressured at school. The owner had a change of attitude once he signed his contract, which was another lesson he learned. He was all smiles, he knew Sean's past, but that was the past and they could get around that; that's what he said. He was questioned about his cars, his jewelry, his cloths and whatever. After awhile, it started bothering him, because he felt as though, he was continuously drilling him. He was real live wolf in sheep's clothing. His advice to anyone, especially the hard working people trying to get ahead, trying to go to school, yet have to work fulltime to maintain; read the fine print in any contract you sign. Even if it's for an appliance, always read the contract thoroughly. He had a clause that stated if you missed more than 120 hours he charged you $4.25 for each hour. If you started in his school and went somewhere else, you still had to pay. To Cat, this was live gangster stuff.

As time went on, the pressure from the church got to him also. He had family members that went to the same church he was attending at the time. He still remained committed, during that time, I believe he was tithing over $100 per week. He was asked to take an office within the church, and he just couldn't see where he could fit anything else into his schedule. He was trying to stay focused on his ultimate goals. As it was, it seemed he was late for everything. They were trying to force him to attend Sunday evening services and Friday night services, quoting the scripture, "forsake not to assemble yourselves together," literally taking contents out of scripture. People can drive you right out of the church pressuring you. While he was away, he studied very hard and he knew the Word. Because of how he had changed, a lot of people could not believe how he had changed from darkness to light. His peers looked at him a different way, and he loved it. He was an example, without even knowing it. He just told them, "it's not me, it's Jesus." His advice to them was to stay away from knuckleheads, selling and using drugs, because when you fall, you fall hard. When you flirt with these things, they take control. He can recall Pastor Fields once telling him that you can't ride with the devil, the devil will ride you. On a few occasions, He was asked to speak on panel discussions, where there were a number of speakers who spoke on a topic, given five to ten minutes each. After a few times out, his pastor approached him about it. He told him that he did not give him permission or he didn't ordain him a minister. That took everything out of him. He felt worthless, as far as being able to go out and do what God wanted him to do. He already was hurt behind the church not coming through for him as promised while he was incarcerated. Like I said before, there were a lot of promises made that weren't kept. This is the reason he was more determined to give back, and one way was by visiting the prisons, helping those in need. He knew what it was like, so he felt it was his duty to try to get there to help his brothers out the best way he could.

One day he went to a halfway house in Trenton to visit his man Nasheed, who had been on the run for seven years. They were real tight. He had had saved his life one day. Cat helped his mom bail him out in '89. When he got out, he gave him his money back and "poof", he was gone. They couldn't catch him. He'd come in town to see his mom and kids and take off again. He was taken into custody when he came to town for his mother's funeral. On the way home, he stopped by his man Rasheem's place. He said, "come out to the garage, I got something to show you." He had a motorcycle... Cat was pressed, with his double breasted suit on and lizards. He said, "here put these on," and handed him a pair of sneakers. The last time he rode was at the age of sixteen on a dirt bike. He had a rush, remembering the good old days. When he got home, he found out a friend of his had a bike for sale for $2500 with only 5200 miles on it. It was a Yamaha Seka 200, yellow. He told Cat the first time he rode it, he went around a corner, slide in some dirt, and never got on it again. They worked out a deal, and thirty days later it was his. He called his man Rasheem to tell him. He laughed and said, "You don't stop until you get what you set out to get, you're something else." One day Cat was riding with a few others, DB had advised him not to buy this particular bike because he said it wasn't fast enough. They were riding own to Wildwood. The fastest he had gotten it up to was 130 mph. So they were cruising 75 to 85 mph, and once they got to a certain point, out of police range, Fox started acting up. He was riding in the back with Sean. Fox switched over to the passing lane, dropped down two gears and took off. The rest of them followed. Steve was on a CX11, DB was riding a CBR900 and Fox was riding a GXR750. They all left him; all he could see were their tail lights. He was running as fast as he could, not getting over 130 mph. Pretty soon, they just disappeared. He caught up at a toll both. Steve took off his helmet and screamed, "195 baby once" Cat said, "oh my God." Fox had hit 165 and DB 175 mph. Steve said he was going for 200. He knew right then that he had to get a new bike. DB warned him not to get it in the first place. During the rest of the trip, these cats had to literally pull over to the side of the road and wait for him. He told them he felt like riding his bike into an eighteen wheeler, he was so embarrassed.

Cat rode after work and on Sundays after church. One day he told Fox that he wanted to buy another bike, so he told him he'd sell him his GXL750 They worked out a deal. Cat sold his bike to his brother, and bought his. It was faster and prettier. Once he got it, drama started jumping off at school. Like he said earlier, the owner had a problem with him. There were two other students who had been to prison. He managed to get rid of them, and I believe he wanted Cat out too. My firm belief is, he couldn't because during that time, Cat was walking with the Lord. He had an attendance problem, so he really worked that against him.

He pulled Cat into the office again, questioning him. This time he didn't pull any punches. He went right to the point. He asked, "What exactly is it you're trying to imply?" He looked at him stunned, like he couldn't believe what he just said. Cat went on, "look my man, I work six day, and if I want to buy a new car, new cloths, new jewelry or a motorcycle, then I'll buy it. My business with you is paying my tuition. You can drive up here in your Lexus, or your Jeep Cherokee, or your motorcycle. You can sit behind your desk in your nice suits wearing your $5000 ring on your finger. When I come here with the same, I must be doing something wrong to get it. I know what you're trying to imply and you're dead wrong." He gave him his little threats, and Cat said, "I'm going to get my license one way or another, whether it's here, Votech or wherever." He really burnt him up, but being in that situation with him, gave him more drive to go after more. He wanted to show him that every black kid that something doesn't necessarily have to be doing something wrong to get it.

Because of all the drama, problems and frustration he was going through in his personal, as well as his business life, the pressures of life were getting to him. Riding in the wind became therapy for him. The day he bought the new bike, he ended up on Main Street and his wife came up. She said to him, "Since you can spend $3500 or $4000, whatever you spend, (speaking of his new bike) I want a 2ct anniversary ring. They went to the jewelry store, she showed what she wanted, and he told her that she can have it but it will probably be around Christmas time. She said, "I'm just telling you what I want, you're just not going to get me anything." He said, "Alright, no problem." One of his boys had taken his son Sean with him. They disappeared and didn't tell him where they were going. Tara was ready to leave, Sean told her not to leave yet, that he would be right back. So he went up to the Rialto and on his way back, she's pulling off laughing. She knew that if he had Sean with him he wouldn't be able to ride that night. So he was mad about that. When his man got back, he told him to take him back to his mom and dad's house. While they were gone, she came back arguing. He said, "don't play games with me". He was mad and wouldn't talk to her. She was yelling from across the street, so he turned and went to the shop. Main Street was not the place to be arguing, especially about personal family business. She came into the shop trying to talk, so he turned the music on. He said, "I don't want to talk now," and she said, "We're going to talk now." He turned the music up and she was trying to talk over the music. She said, "Oh, you want to ignore and drown me out? I'm sick of you and your boys. When you get time, you can call your boy, the lawyer, and tell him to draw up the papers and I'll sign them." Then she left.

Cat had a customer in the chair, but something told him to go out behind her. There he saw his bike lying on the ground and she was walking away from it. He was so mad, he didn't know whether to go after her or pick up his bike. On of his boys helped him pick it up, all the time rubbing it in his face. There was a cop sitting on his bicycle who rode up laughing and asked if he wanted to sign a complaint. "Real funny, sign a complaint against his wife." They thought this was cute. One of Cat's partner's pop was across the street. He said, "man she didn't push your bike down, she kicked your bike down, like errrrrr." He said, "You ain't right." Fortunately there wasn't too much damage. The pipe took most of the fall and the front brake was bent. He was just so upset that he asked her again to help him get it and she wouldn't, and now she did this out of spite, I guess because he was able to get it anyway. So now, this created another situation.

A very close friend of his, Marilyn Eason, who he calls his second mom, allowed him to put his bike in her garage, since he didn't want to keep it outside. She and her husband Quientin, have been real close friends to Sean and his family over the years. He used to go buy and talk to her all the time about different things. She knew when he was out on the bike because his car would be parked in her driveway. As time went by, he started riding more. His man would come by early on Sunday morning, and they were gone. So that meant, he wasn't attending morning churches services. Now he was on a new roll, out on Sunday morning, relaxing, him and the wind. He found himself making excuses for his actions like, "Sunday is my only day off," or "I have all this drama in my life, I may as well go out and relax." One Sunday when he went by her house, she called for him to come, she wanted to talk to him for a minute. All she said was, "Sean, don't let that bike take the place of god." He said, "I know."

Around this time he was finishing up at the school. It took him twenty two months to finish an eleven month course, mainly from being hardheaded and stubborn. In addition, he had to pay $2500 extra for overtime hours. He had 453 hours he had done while in the State prison system, but those hours couldn't be counted toward the requirement for State Board. He always thought the director of the school had something to do with that. They were on a strict probation preparing to go before the State Board. He was called into the office again, and this time this man said, "You know what, for this whole year, we've been batting 100%. (Meaning graduates) I think you're going to be the one that messes up that 100%." Cat said, "Thanks a lot."

He ran into one of his partners on Mother's Day when he was out riding. He had just come home from prison and his mother suggested he go see Sean. They began talking and he gave him the best advice he could, like staying focused. He told him how he got as far as he did, by going to school, work and church. They talked, but he really wasn't feeling Sean because he was Muslim. A couple weeks later, Cat was on his way to church with the family. They were riding up Adams Avenue and ran into him. He stopped the car and he came over. He thought that if he saw he was for real, that this is what he does, maybe it would convince him that he was speaking the truth. When he came over to the car, he started to speak to Sean but stopped and said to his wife, "Happy Mother's Day." The look she gave him wasn't too friendly. Cat went to the church and told her he was leaving and to page him when she was ready. She said, "oh, you're not going to church today?" He said, "I'm going to church, but not with you today." They were on Pacific Avenue, and out in front of everybody, she got out of the car and slammed the door with both hands. Again his blood pressure shot up. He let his son out of the car and told him to go with his mother. She brought him back, put him in the car, said, "go with your father," and slammed the door again. He then put the car in park, let his son out and told him to go with his mother. She came back, since the doors were locked, she started pounding on the roof of the car, and screaming, "I hate you." Deacon Ragland was out there. He said to Sean, "it's not as bad as it seems." He could see that he had tears in his eyes.

That was a big pill to swallow. They talked and agreed to go to counseling. Of course, everything was his fault.

He was blamed for everything. So he said, "You're right, it's all my fault. You're the perfect wife that God dropped out of heaven. I came along and messed up everything." She replied, "Now you're trying to be sarcastic." To him, counseling was like a big joke. He was doing the best he could after prison, it was the best he had to give at the time. He had all this drama at his home, trying to ignore it, yet trying to deal with the whole situation. Most cats that come home from prison don't make it past ninety days. Statistics show that most either get a parole violation or a new charge. They were dealing with other problems, such as control games being played. He begged her not to play those games with him, and she would just say, "I'm not playing games."

Chapter Six

When Cat came home in 1996, He had a new respect for freedom, being released on parole didn't matter to him much at all, since he's been monitored more than half of his life at that time anyway, but one thing he knew for sure was being incarcerated was one place he didn't want to be. Everything seemed strange when he first came home, everything looked different. He tried to prepare himself for society as best he could. He thought of all the basic things he would need before he came home. A couple of sweat suits, a couple of suits, sneakers, jewelry, and fortunately for him his wife purchased a townhouse three months before he came home. The house was solely in his wife's name, the state of New Jersey wouldn't allow him to buy, co-sign or lease anything in the state, how about that? His plan was to get a good cliental start from cutting hair then finish school for cosmetology and get his license. One day, in 1994 down Bordentown, he cut 36 heads in one day. It didn't take a rocket scientist to do the math, so his barbering career started right then and there.

Things didn't look so promising in the first shop, he walked in and made $35 the first three days in the shop. Tara had almost no patience at all, she told him, "babe, I know this is something you really want to do, but you have to get another job somewhere until you start making some money." Of course this was not something that he wanted to hear, but he used the gift of understanding and put himself in her position. Even though he was home now she knew what bills looked like every month when they came in. So Sean moved on and got started somewhere else which was a totally different ball game.

Early September 1997 his grandmother passed away. Everyone was sad, he knew he would miss her very much but she told him she was ready to go. Every since he came home from prison he tried to spend as much time as he could with her, and make her as comfortable as he could. Ginger-ale & Sherbet was her normal request. He tried to stop by every morning on his way to school, sometime he would lay on the floor, and she would tell him about her life. She often told him how proud she was of him, but he could always tell himself by the look in her eyes and the smile she always gave him. His only concern was if she was in any pain, he couldn't stand the thought of a woman who has been through so much suffering in life, to suffer at all in death, not as much as he loved her.

Well the very day he had her body laid to rest, and said their final goodbyes, their family gathered over his aunt's house. He had just bought his first motorcycle a couple of months before that, so he went home and got his bike, and everyone wanted to ride. So he took his cousin Wayne for a ride, they shot down the street at about 70-75 miles per hour. Cat saw a tractor out of the corner of his eye off to his right about twenty feet away and I don't think he saw him because he made no attempt to stop. He was going out of one yard across the street to another. He tried to slow down but he was just going too fast. He had to swerve around the back of this tractor. I mean barely missing the back by inches. So much flashed across his mind in that one split second it's undesirable. He thought about this cat named Leo he knew who got killed this summer of 1996 right down the street from where he was at, on a bike. In one split second about a month later, he went for a ride to Wildwood and the cat's he was riding with were crazy. These jokers were running

165 to 195 miles per hour, they literally disappeared on him. His little bike wasn't fast enough, he was doing 135 miles per hour but it just wasn't enough. So he had to get him a new bike. Bigger, stronger & much faster. He wanted to get a brand new bike, but his wife wouldn't co-sign so he bought his boy fox's bike off of him. A GSXR750.

Going into 1998 was promising, things were going very well, Cat was finally almost finished with cosmetology school, and his wife was pregnant with his youngest son Malachi, but everything wasn't so well spiritually on the inside of him. He was slowly drifting away from God, and looking for God to bring him through his circumstances like before. He started just looking at all of his problems. He started looking at everything around him. He started seeing the fake and the frauds, the liars and cons. He wanted to go at this thing a whole nother way. He couldn't help but remember the thing that happened in his life. He had seen one of his cousins one day at a renaissance party, he was sitting in his Benz you know, he got lucky, caught a break, and somebody helped him out.

All right, Cat asked him to order him some rims for his car. I mean he got 4 or 5 cars all tricked up, he knew they'd give him a better deal than they'd give him. This joker laughed and said, "I can't do that." Cat laughed and walked away and said, "yeah, I bet you can't." It's funny how quickly people forget about you, and the things you done for them. Now this boy was brought up in church all his life, his daddy is a preacher. He started hustling, detailing cars, the joker used to do some at his house. His sister was at that time one of the finest women from this area. Some how she caught the eyes of a very big drug dealer name Larry. Big fat dude, cuz said he weighed about 400lbs. This cat was so big she said she went to see him in NY one day and he couldn't fit in her car.

Cat told her he wanted to meet this joker, he might be

the connection he needed. She replied, "no- no this guy is dangerous Sean, some guy stole 75,000 from him and he had his hands cut off. He said, "It would have been too easy to kill him so I want him to suffer, I want him to think about my money he stole every time someone has to feed him or wipe his ass." So she said no. Well her brother started getting real familiar with this cat over the phone, and some how convinced him to front him some cocaine. Now once he has it the boy didn't know what to do with it, so who does he call? You guessed it!, he called o'l cuz. Cat went to his house to give the joker the help he needed to get started, he just couldn't believe he had drugs in his fathers house, so he asked him why?, and he looked Sean dead in his eyes, and said because he can't trust anybody to do anything for him.

He didn't know it, but that was the most important lesson of the game. So he's making his moves and a couple weeks later he comes to him with a list of names of cats that owe him money that refuse to pay him. So who do you think starts pushing up for him, and his money, yeah you know who, but let them tell it, it's all different. Cat could've gotten killed or killed one of them if the situation got heated over some drug money that wasn't his in the first place, but he wasn't ever looking at it like that. All Cat knew was these jokers are only doing this to cuz, because they know he wasn't a fighter. He comes to him scared to death cause he owes this big dope boy some money, and he has to pay him, so what does he do? He helps his cousin, and what does he do? Catches "Selective Memory".

Meaning he selects what he wants to remember. Cat used to see his daddy jump up, and down in the pulpit and say, "give and it shall be given unto you press down, shaken up, shall the lord give unto you" "we need to have another offering, we need you right now church!." If you ask them for help now, the answer is, "I can't do it." Now I don't have a problem with I can't do it if it were true, but when you tell family no, and strangers yes, you have forgotten where you came from, and you are fake and a liar. They need to examine themselves. There's a big difference between I can't and I don't want to. Almost a much bigger difference when you were begging for years, and receiving. Now you can't help the ones who helped you at one time or another. He remembers a scripture that his Uncle use to quote that he thinks he forgot. "What shall a man profit if he gains the whole world and lose his sole?" At one time he was told by this preacher that if we go to the movies, listen to worldly music, or if women wore pants, they were going to hell. It seems now that he can make a profit off of it, now it's just a job. He talks more about his money in the pulpit than Jesus. He use to hear him preach on the subject of a Camel having a better chance of making it through the eye of a needle than a rich man making it to heaven. So Cat just sits back and watch, study like a chess player, and watch the ones who are humble and have money as well as the ones who change faces.

Then he understood what the scripture meant. Cat made a big mistake shortly after that in '97, he took his eyes off of God and started focusing on other things that were pleasing to a man's eyes, the temptation was so great he could understand the position Adam was in "in the Garden of Eden". The temptation that seemed almost unbearable, and seemed to be so sweet. Every Christian will be tempted one time or another, and trust me when I tell you it's best to be ready when it comes, cause if you get caught slipping it's very dangerous fighting a war with no weapons. Not realizing the traps that were being set before him, or realizing how far away he was slipping from the presence and power of God, He started living real reckless and dangerous. He got involved in a few things he shouldn't have gotten into, but we all make bad decisions sometimes, and I mean everybody.

He just thanked God that he showed him what he was doing, and the consequences of his actions, then it was up to him to make a decision. Does he keep doing something he knows is not right, and can put himself in jeopardy of losing his life or freedom, or walk away. Ever since he was a kid he had a lot of negativity spoken over his life. He was told he'll never be anybody, he'll end up dead, or in jail the rest of his life before he turned 21; for a while that thing really bothered him. Right in the beginning of '98, he just finished Cosmetology school, and before he left the school he was told by the owner, that he couldn't see him being successful in this business or in life. Cat told him thanks for the confidence and have a nice day.

He really didn't know who was hotter himself, for the owner trying to belittle him, or the owner for Cat insulting him so nicely without revealing his true feelings. One thing is for sure he knew he was going to prove him wrong. So the first thing he had to do was pass the State Board examination. The owner of his school told him every person sent from their school passed, and he thinks Cat will be the one to mess up that 100% rating average. You know who passed the test? Then o'boy wanted to shake his hand, but he told him to kiss his a**. He owed his cousin Lou Lou a lot, because she was his model for the state board and he had to chip her up a little something, but it was for his license, and her hair did grow back, but he did want her to know how much that meant to him. Shortly after all of this he found himself being numb to sin, and all he cared about was his motorcycle, and at that time he was keeping his bike over a good friend of his, he always called his second mom, Marilyn has been a friend of their family for years. Marilyn knew when he was out on his bike, because his car would be parked in her driveway and he wouldn't be in the house. So one Sunday when he came to get his bike, she said, "hey son how are you doing? I haven't seen you in a while."

She then said, "I see you've been riding a lot on Sunday". She then asked him when is the last time he was in church? The reason she said this is because he was on her heart real heavy while she was in prayer. Before he left she told him that she loved him, and not to put the motorcycle in God's place. Subconsciously that's exactly what was going down. Later on that week on Thursday April 2, 1996, while out riding with his brother-in-law, enjoying nature's smooth & lovely breezes, Cat watched his brother run a stop sign a lot of people ignored, and almost got smashed out by a 18 wheeler, he was in the back and could see the whole incident. My man didn't see the truck or know the truck had the right away. He knew it was either or, because he made no attempt to slow down or stop. He looked at this picture and he sees a big truck slamming on his brakes, tires just burning smoke everywhere. The driver was so shaken, he looked over at Cat sitting at the corner while both of them were shaking their heads. He just waved him through. So Cat took off down the street to catch him at the next corner.

He pulled up on the side of him, took his helmet off, and said, "Now tell me you didn't see that truck?" He said he didn't. He replied, "you're lying Mother F*****!, you almost got smashed out boy!, you better watch what you are doing, and stop playing!" So they bounced out to Hamilton to a cycle shop. On the way back riding down route 322, two minutes away from where he lives; a car makes an illegal turn at a stop light after missing his turn at a jug handle. He put on no left signal, he just cut right in front of him, and came to a complete stop, maybe 9 to 12 feet away from him.

Chapter Seven

It was shock and anger that sprung him up so quickly while screaming, "I can't believe this shit! – oh God, look at my bike!"

Cat's brother–in–law came running across the street crying, "Reef, Reef!" "Look at your ass," "get down man!" At the time the shock was fading and so was he. He actually heard the wife of the driver trying to tell the police he hit them, as if it was his fault; and once again the range of injustice rose up in his throat. The excitement and anger, along with his injuries started taking its toll on him. He started hyperventilating as he slowly fell into an unconscious state of mind. He began seeing clips of his life quickly flashing in his mind. He then thought of how he had been "back sliding" for too long, and it was then that he truly felt a strong fear of death. He knew he wasn't anywhere near being ready for his judgment day.

So right away, he knew what had to be done. I know everyone can relate to what I am talking about, because everyone in this life has been there. All he could say to himself at that moment was, "oh God, if I ever needed you the most, it would be right now!" He prayed, "Dear God, I know that I haven't been living right, and I ask that you please forgive me?" "God, please don't take me now; please give me another chance."

As he was being transported to the hospital, he truly didn't feel that he was going to make it. The medics wanted to take him to Mainland Hospital; however he requested to go to Shore Hospital, since his wife worked there. As they vigorously headed for Shore Hospital, a thousand of thoughts entered his mind, but the one thought that kept ringing in his ears were the words of Maryland, saying; "don't let that bike in the place of God, I only warn you because I love you son." Tears ran down his face, when he thought of how selfish he had become. A lot of people never realized that the consequences of their actions affect many others. After arriving at Shore Hospital, the paramedics wheeled him into the emergency unit, and there was "momma" waiting, big belly and all. When Cat looked into her tear filled eyes, he felt even worse. He couldn't imagine what ran through her mind after she received the call. Once again, he knew she didn't deserve to go through this, especially after he promised her that he was done with bikes. He was quickly treated and released from the hospital that same day.

One of his partners named "G-money," was driving home from work heading down route 322 and saw Cat's bike banged up on the mall lot. He immediately called him, and he explained to him what had happened, and asked him to pick up his bike.

Old boy went and got Cat's bike and came to see him. He had bandages everywhere, and this joker looked at him and said, "don't let this accident scare you man, get back on that horse!" The following day, which was Friday, He had to go into work since he didn't have any disability insurance. So there he was wrapped up like a mummy, in the shop, cutting hair as he experienced excruciating pair! The road rash was so bad, that every time he moved, it hurt somewhere! Every time he changed his bandages, some skin would peel off. It seemed as if the healing process would take forever. And what made matters worse was when his wife would remark, "yeah, I bet you wished you would have listened to me now, don't you?"

And all he could say was, "I know, I know!" Well, as time went on, the orthopedic doctor said it was nothing else to be done, and the rest of his healing would take place naturally. So like so many of us do, he believed the doctor, while his body was telling him something else. He had never experienced this kind of pain before, so he didn't know how much time to allow for the healing process to be complete. However, when he began to feel worse as time went on, He instinctively knew that something was terribly wrong. Just as he suspected, the quick medical attention that he had received was just that, quick! No MRI's or "cat" scans had been taken. To make a long story short, there was never a real thorough examination done.

Chapter Eight

Quite often, since the accident, Cat has experience horrific flash backs and a lot sleepness nights. He feels very ashamed of the scars that remain. Each time someone looks at them he gets bombarded with questions such as, "what happened to you?" Or "yo!, were you afraid?" Then there were certain other things that he would hear that would bring up that horrible experience. Since his scars had such an emotional affect on him. His attorney suggested that he consult with a plastic surgeon, who explained to him that surgery would not benefit him, it would only cause the scars to be more visible. Once again, Cat felt that he was faced wit adversity. When he found out that he would have a permanent reminder for the rest of his life, his blood pressure shot straight up. The anger that he felt from within almost uncontrollable. At this point, the attorney suggested that he see a therapist, after consulting the therapist, he was told that he has a lot of anger and bitterness inside of him. "Oh", he thought, "no kidding!, I would have never figured that out!"

Cat looked at this person, who in his mind probably never had a fight in his life, never wanted for much, college graduate, silver spoon and the whole nine yards. The only thing he could think was, "this guy is a joke." And the only thing Cat could say to him was, "do you really think so?"

Surprisingly enough, he continued to see him, hoping that maybe he could offer him some invaluable insight.

Needless to say, the questions kept getting worse and worse. He told Cat he was going to help him deal with the emotional pain cause by the scars. At this point, he told him that the only way he could possibly help him was to take the scars away. He then replied, "I can't do that." Cat then responded by saying, "then you can't help me." There was nothing in the world that man could say to him to change how he feels about those scars. He has come to the reality that he may have to continue to look at them and live with them for the rest of his life.

After a few months had past, Cat received a check for the damages to his motorcycle, along with a letter from the insurance company that explained that their client was 100% liable for the accident.

Ironically so, right after cashing the check, he purchased another bike. He had it for approximately (1) month when one of his boys who he had grown up with and had finished serving prison time with, approached him and said, "I heard you're selling your bike?" He replied by saying, "yeah, I am." This young cat then proceeded to ask if he could buy it. He told him, "you can buy it if you have, $5,500. Old boy told him meet him around the projects in 10 minutes.

Cat went around there, and to his amazement, this joker peeled off $4,500, and then told him that he would give him the rest of his money on that coming Friday. Cat then said, "No way buddy!" Then he said, "I'm not good for a grand?" Cat then proceeded to laugh in his face. He explained to him that it was nothing personal, but the bottom line is by being the drug dealer that he is, if he gets knocked," then he won't get paid! So cat suggested that he hand over the chain that was hanging around his neck. This cat looked at him and said, "yo, are you stupid?" Cat just bought this joint, and he paid $1,800 for it. He never winked, blinked, smiled or anything. He just firmly said to him, "do you want this bike or not?"

Cat then went on to say, "If you do, we're closing this deal today! Right now!" As he looked at him, my man stared at the bike as if it were a thick well-cooked juicy steak, prepared to perfection for a starving man! This bike was so pretty, until it was unreal. My man then looked up at Cat, took his chain off of his neck and handed it over. He couldn't walk around with this joker's chain on. He eventually traded in the chain in order to put a down payment on the ring, and bought him another bike. The accident really took a lot out of him, but because of his love for motorcycles, he kept a bike. However, whenever he rode his bike, he would always think about the many stupid mistakes that could fatally injure or kill him for being an unprotected cyclist. These fearful thoughts eventually caused him to ride his bike less and less. When he purchased the second bike, he soon discovered the very next day that the cycle shop owner had sold him a bike with bald tires and a damaged transmission! He called him immediately and told he told Cat that the bike had been sold to him on an "as is" basis. Cat told him he had $4,500 down as a down payment on a brand new bike. This sucker looked at him as if he had five heads and spoke a language that he had never heard before. Then he said, "if you want to trade the bike in that you just purchased yesterday, I'll give you $3,000." Word is bond, when he said that to him, Cat thought he was definitely going back to jail. He started getting real nervous when he saw the anger level rise up in him. He began to back up, Cat said, "you know what Bicthal, you will pay for this, I promise you!" "I'm going to tell all my boys how you get down and I want my transmission fixed right because it is under warranty!" He looked at him and said, "as you know, there will be a $300 deductible for any major work done on you bike."

Cat then replied, "keep the bike!. I'll be calling my attorney! Now the negotiation process starts. He couldn't believe this "cat" was striving to get more money out of him. He ended up getting (2) new tires and a new transmission for the price of (1) tire.

After a young sister came in to pay on a layaway for her boyfriend, (a $10,000 bike), Cat proceeded to tell her about what he had just gone through. The receptionist at the bike shop immediately got up from her chair at her desk and walked toward him. She then said in a very sarcastic tone, "oh no Sean, she is taken," He then replied, "I'm not trying to pick her up, I'm making her aware of the poor customer service that I received minutes before she arrived." Needless to say, after having this conversation, the young sister asked for her deposit of $3,000 back. After this took place he left the shop with a very satisfied smile on his face. However, the threat of exposing his shady deals and true colors to his dogs, and the call to his attorney, ended getting Cat two new high performance tires and a rebuilt transmission for $180. He didn't want to handle this situation by using threats, but he had his money and he felt that by pursuing this matter legally, could have taken years before it was resolved. So he chalked it up as a loss, and told Bitchal that he owed him one and he meant that! Cat's partner "G-money" told him why he didn't bother to deal with these cats. He said, "look at how they did you dog?" that "motherfucker" sold you a bike with bald tires on it, and he couldn't care less if you died out there, as long as he got your money, that's all that mattered.

Not too long after that, he had an opportunity to buy another GSXR 750, and yes, you guessed it, he also had a buyer for the 2x6. He sold it to his God brother for $4,500 and paid $4,700 for the new bike. About three weeks later, someone hit "lil bro" and he lost about $4,500 so he asked him to buy the bike back for $2,000, so he jumped on it because he knew he could get $4,000 for it easy. He then called Cat back two days later and told him that he needed the bike back. He was waiting for this young cat's call. He called and told Cat that he was waiting for the money. Lil bro told him he would give him $2,500. "I'm like you" he said, "I got it sold for $4,000." He went on to say, "Look, you're going to make $500 in less than 48 hours." Cat knew that "hit" really hurt him, so he let it go. A few days later he told him what he had done and he was hotter than fish grease! He had a partner in "Philly" who wanted a bike, and was trading a '95 ford explorer, which he had sold before he got it.

A few days later, while thinking about everything that had just transpired, he realized that he had made $10,000 in one day. Cat started thinking, "there has to be people in this world that have made $10,000 on one day?" and he made it legally! He then thought, "Man, that's 3.6 million a year!" Then he went on to think, "$10,000 a week is a half million a year." However, it's a fact, "you must crawl before you walk in this life time." So he set his eyes on $10,000 a month first. Supply and demand has always been a part of his life, and everybody else's for that matter, so he had to find out what was in demand, then find out how he was going to supply it!

One day sitting in his barber chair, was one of his faithful customers who had moved to Southern New Jersey from New York. He told Cat that he and his family decided to stay there and purchase a home once their lease had expired. He then jokingly said, "I'll sell you my house, " He very quickly replied, "okay!" At this point in time, Cat was really feeling some kind of way about some of the decisions he'd been making. All he could think In his mind was, "man Sean, how could you let yourself get in this type of position when you know your chess game is better than this." Then he got a few very serious warnings where he could possibly see death or jail and God knows he didn't want either. So, his intuitions kept telling him the only answer to this madness was to stop what he was doing.

He always got complaints on his attire, but lately a lot of his customers and his youth would ask him where and how much? Well, you know him, a light came on in his head immediately, which gave him the idea to contact the owners of the stores where he purchases his outfits and negotiate. In no time flat, he was in business. He was making anywhere from $400 to $750 a week extra. Everything was flowing like gravy.

He's still constantly thinking about his spiritual life and how much he changed. He knew he was doing wrong and sometimes he couldn't control his wrongfulness. He got so comfortable in his sinful way of being that it stated controlling him. His God brother, Shon-Don said to him one day while looking him straight in his eyes, "Sean. Word is bond man, you wilding!" His response was "man, I'm cool" But immediately after he said that, Cat had to really check himself out. So he started to take an inventory from the time he returned from jail up to this point in his life. He couldn't say that he was pleased with some of his decisions, but he vowed to change them.

Once he decided to retreat, analyze and regroup, he started seeing a lot of things happening. He began seeing how "jokers" fall off, make mistakes and get caught slipping. It hurts him to the heart when he warn these "jokers" and it happens to them, and all he can say to them while visiting them at the county jail or at a funeral is, it didn't have to be this way. However, the guys who are fortunate to answer him back, can only say, "I know Sean, I know!"

Remember Cast's faithful customer, I mentioned

earlier in this chapter who he offered to sell his house to? Well he came into the shop during the early part of May '99 and said their lease will expire in July of '99 and wanted to know when he could take a look at his house. He asked him, "for what?" He then said, "oh, you don't want to sell it to me now?" Cat said, "oh yeah, well let me check with my wife and we'll set something up." When he arrived home that evening, he told "momma" "stark looking for a new house, and make sure it has extra room for a pool table."They contacted their real estate broker and made it clear that they were looking for another home with room for a pool table and two floor was a must. In the process of all this, Cat was asked to go on a trip to Cancun Mexico, so the peer pressure was on. However, he owed it to his wife to take her on a nice vacation since they didn't have a honeymoon. He knew that if he had gone on a trip like that without her, he would have never heard the end of that. So, the two of them took a nice little vacation to Jamaica and renewed their vows at the same time. It was a very special and romantic time in their lives, just him "momma" and the boys. Cat really wanted to take his two daughters, but their mother wasn't speaking to him, so he was on punishment for being daddy, until she saw fit.

At the end of may '99 about one week before they were about to leave, all Cat's boys on bikes were getting together to ride to "Philly," so he considered taking that trip with them. It was Friday night, you know, the "plat" up in philly was jumping, then he get's a call from his daughter asking him if they could come over that night. Needless to say, he couldn't turn them down especially hearing the soft beautiful voices of his little girls. He said yes without hesitation, as he was leaving for work, he saw one of the riders standing down the street holding his little girl.

He asked Cat if he was going to roll with the biking crew, he told them he wanted to go, but he had a hot date tonight with his daughters. He then said, "Yeah, I'm trying to get it In now," as he gently kissed his baby's cheek. Cat told him to ride easy.

Early Saturday morning, another one of the "boys" came through the shop with teary eyes and said, Sean, I know you hear about Oshi." He looked up at his man an by the look on his face just about told the story, but his words confirmed his worst fear. A car ran a red light or stop sign, while Oshi was riding a "wheelie>" He asked, "was he still alive?" His boy said, "yeah, but he's in real bad shape"

They supposedly had to cut his legs off, and he broke a lot of bones from the waist up. "Old boy" made it for a week, then he died during surgery. His funeral was three days after their scheduled vacation. Cat new this vacation was very important to Tara. She always said, "You chose your friends before you're family." He never believed this to be true, but if he had postponed their vacation to attend this funeral, he would have never heard the end of that. Then he had to realize that, this wasn't a regular vacation they were planning, it was time to go on their honeymoon that they were never able to and renew their marriage vows. I must admit, I felt really bad on the day of the funeral, but he has to live with his wife for the rest of his life. As soon as they returned from their honeymoon, roughly about two weeks later, Cat received a phone call that his cousin Rease from Hagerstown, MD was killed in a bad motorcycle accident. It was noted that he supposedly was operating the motorcycle a little over 100 mph, and as he proceeded to switch lanes he was hit by an oncoming car. He heard it was a very ugly site. He felt very bad for his cousin, Diane, "I am sure "cuz" never thought he would go out like that!" he thought.

But that's what life is all about, you never know how it will happen. This is why you really must be sure of the things you are doing, and get involved with, because it could mean the difference between life and death.

Several days after his cousin's funeral, he and Tara were scheduled for the closing on the town house, but they were having problems with a slick mortgage broker who really ended up putting the screws to them. It was bad enough that Tara had to find their house on her own, but they had everyone else delaying the deal. It was a good thing Cat knew "Wes" and Charlotte; they were nice enough to let them stay in the house until after their lease was up. Cat hired an attorney toward the end of the deal, and when he came on the scene a lot of things were accomplished!

After getting his attorney involved with the deal, they had the exterior property completely checked out. Unfortunately, it was told to them that their house was contaminated by an oil leakage. After the oil leakage was detected, the EPA department was contacted. Once they get involved, nine times out of ten you almost surely expect some kind of delay or fallen deal. His attorney, whom which he is glad to say his wife was proud of hiring, immediately put his real estate expertise in action. He contacted the seller's lawyer, and no quicker than you can blink you're eyes papers were being faxed back and fourth, then the negotiations were on. He quickly learned a lot about the real estate game, and why it is important to have a lawyer when signing your name to contracts. It's sad to say that more times than one, it's best to get a second opinion even with your attorney. That's why he has (6) attorneys that look after him and his business deals. The seller's lawyer suggested that they escrow him $4,000 towards the clean up of the oil leakage. Cat's lawyer firmly stated that they have the entire spill repaired and cleaned up or they will find another house. When Cat got the word of what he said to them, he asked his lawyer was he out of his mind? He said, "No, not at all, you hired me to protect you and that's what I'm going to do." He then went on to say, "If you go against what I recommend for the contract, I won't represent you." He claimed that he would write a letter addressing him, the seller's lawyer and the Title Company stating that he no longer represents him. Cat's response was "why does it have to be like that?" He asked Cat if he wanted to take a chance on that container being a spill from an oil filling or a leak that could have been there as long as the house? Cat never asked him, but he says he must find out if he is a chess player. He really loved the way he handles his business. He not only represents you, he teaches you about this thing you're getting involved with and the rules that go along with it. Later on as you read this book, you'll find out the temptation was so great that Cat was willing to break the rules and could have possibly put himself in checkmate. So make sure you pay attention and you'll know what I'm talking about. This was the start of a very long process that took a lot of time, patience and legal skills that left him and his family basically homeless for approximately (3) months. It was a very, very difficult moment for Cat. For one, he had to talk his wife into buying the house that seemed to be the ideal house from the description that she found off the internet. However, when they went to see, it was quite the contrary. She was not happy at all, but by Cat being a barber and having customers who are carpenters, plumbers, electricians, principals, doctors, lawyers and every other profession under the sun and I mean every position, he had a different view of the outcome of this house. Needless to say, all of the legal drama didn't help his case at all. He ended up convincing "momma" to trust him and roll with him for at least one year. It was a really trying time all the way up to the last papers at the closing table. However, while negotiations were going on, he had another negotiation going on about his pool table. As soon as they were done closing they immediately went up the street to the billiards store and gave them the last payment owed for his pool table while setting up a delivery date. Out of all his so called "friends" who were supposed to help him move, only six of them showed up to help him, and they were Buzz, Prince, Wafiq, Dave, Rafiq and Ahmad, but they managed to get it all done. Cat's co-worker, who he cut hair with, really understood that this was costing him a lot of money, and he had held him down through thick and thin, and for that he'll be forever grateful. They didn't get along too well in the beginning, but for some strange reason, they bonded like brothers in the end and out of respect, Cat never did anything to cross him, he always kept it real with him. Because of this respect he had shown him, Cat always thought he could trust this dude, and he would never cross him. He loved him as if he were his own brother. However, shortly after he moved into his new house, they were shooting a game of pool with a few other guys when someone made a comment about what he should do in the pool house. So after everyone had finished shooting a game of pool, "lil bro" made everyone leave something for the house. They were used to shooting pool until three to five thirty in the morning almost every night for about a month after they moved in. 'Lil bro's" wife had a little something to say about this. However, what Cat's wife and other wives and girlfriends didn't understand was when they were shooting pool and having a good time amongst good friends, time didn't matter. So one day "lil bro" told Cat he needed to get a clock for the pool house. He told him "you need to get a clock for the pool house "cuz", I'm home". He said, "you're right, I'll do that!" Before "lil bro" left that night, he made sure that he took a collection from Hank G, Luck, Old T, Shylynn, Jerry and Sonnie, for a housewarming gift just for the pool house. With the money he collected he purchased a marble green clock to match the marble green pool table. When his dad saw this marble clock, he said "I like that cat, he's got style" and Cat replied, that's his name, "styles."

During this period of time, Cat and his wife were experiencing rough and turbulent waters, to the point that they weren't speaking to each other. He heard her mention something about a doctor's appointment, but he didn't pay it much attention. Her appointment was on a Friday. Early Saturday morning, he was getting ready for work and while walking through the dining room, "momma" asked him "why do we argue whenever we start to talk to each other?" He replied, "Because you don't know how to talk to me." She asked him to sit down and listen to what she had to say! She looked at him, and started to speak as a tear ran down her face, she then said, "yesterday when I went to the doctor's office" He said, "wait a minute, let me sit down." His wife then told him that the doctor had found a large mass in her throat, and as the words fell off her lips her eyes fluttered up with tears. In a delayed reaction, reality hit him, then it was clear to him exactly what his mate was saying. He quickly had to catch his emotions, so at least one of them could be strong at this point. He tried to convince her not to think the worse when they really don't know what it is that they were dealing with. He promised her that they would obtain the best doctors to take good care of her. Shortly after, he proceeded to work, and as he drove down the street a million thoughts ran through his mind. He thought about their first kiss, the first time they made love, the first time he broke her heart. He thought about their wedding, then he thought about their last conversation before he went to court and got railroaded, and how he kissed her forehead as she slept and told her it was going to be over today, and never came home. He thought about the true love "momma" proved over the four long very rough (4) years of being incarcerated, which happen to be the first four years of their marriage. By the time he reached work, he knew the reality of a serous problem was visible on his outward appearance when one of his co-workers asked him if he was ok. He then proceeded to set up his clippers while trying very hard to hold his composure, but he just broke down right there in the barber shop. He couldn't fight the tears any longer.

As many times as he thought their relationship might be over, as many times he thought he wanted a divorce, the very thought of his wife being taken away from him gave him chills like he never felt in his life. At this point, the only thing he could say is "God" "Please, not like this." It had been a very long time since he truly prayed, but this one broke him to his knees. After getting himself back together, he decided that this battle was too tough for him to fight alone. Not only did he have to deal with his own personal problems in his everyday life, he knew at this point his entire life was about to change. They started seeing all kinds of doctors, and "momma" had to have a lot of tests done. In the end, she was diagnosed with cancer. It was in the early stages, but still very serious. The financial pressures that he was going through, along with the best he could do with helping "momma" at home started to get real intense when outside voices started telling him what he should and should not do. His whole thing was, he knew his wife was sick, and needs his help around the house and things of that nature, but he also knew just because she was sick didn't mean that the bills were going to wait until "momma" got better. Everybody had opinions for what Sean can do, but no one had a game plan for these damn bills, So he did what he knew he had to do. As time went on, he watched his queen go through many ups and downs, and really felt bad watching her go through this. This experience has really taught him how to be sympathetic of people with life threatening illnesses. And his heart truly goes out to them. Half way through "momma's" treatment, he thought about a reverse situation after analyzing their financial status. I mean, it had only been two years ago he could have lost his life or he could have been handicapped himself by messing around with a big toy, which was his motorcycle. He is the bread winner of the family and they lost so much of an income with "momma" coming out of work. Cat thought, man, if it had been his income that was affected like this, they would be in trouble! Trouble to the point of possibly losing what they have, and he worked too hard to lose all of this. So he said to himself, "we must get a solid investment that will generate a solid monthly income. That was the plan, but not such an easy task to achieve. Cat tried to keep his word with his wife in spite of everything that was going on, he still tried to get that house together little by little. Fortunately for them that they have some very good friends who really cared about his family and him. During that winter and spring of 2000, Cat was really starting to feel the financial pressure. His mortgage was almost double on his new house, and he had new bills that he didn't have to pay in the town house. He knew he had a lot of work to do at the house, and he basically lost three incomes and was stressed out. Then he was riding down the street with a million thoughts going through his mind and he got a call on his cell phone. A soft voice came across the line and politely said hello Mr. Timberlake, this is Mrs. Molock, and I'm calling to find out if you are still interested in purchasing the property. He almost cried right there in his car. He pulled over to the side of the road and explained to Mrs. Molock that at the present time he was broke. She said, "oh my God, what happened?" So he explained his entire situation to her, then asked if she could give him some to find out what he needed to buy the property and put everything together. She asked him how much time did he need? He replied about three or four months. She got quiet for a moment, then said okay Mr. Timberlake, I'll wait three or four months for you, but the only thing I ask is that you keep in touch and keep me informed on what's going on. He thanked her for working with him and assured her that he wouldn't let her down. He told her that he would meet with her at least once a week to show his interests in the building as well as his sincerity.

So, immediately after this conversation, he called his mortgage broker, to find out what kind of programs were available to him, and how much money he would need to get this building. From that point, a very serious chess game had begun. He didn't know where he was going to get this cash from, but he knew he had to get it. He had seen that kind of money before, so he knew he could get it again. Cat admits, it was not an easy task, but because of his determination to obtain this property, He refused to be denied by anything or anyone. He had to get focused man!

At that time, he had only $800 to his name, a sick wife, an unfinished house and a lot of stress. But he knew that he needed this property in order to have solid foundation. He remembered a scripture in the bible that spoke about a man who built his house on sand and another who built his on solid foundation. When a strong wind and storm came along, one of the houses stood and the other fell. It shouldn't take a rocket scientist to figure out which one fell and which one stood. When he considered his financial position during those tough times, he felt that his house was sitting on a sandy foundation. He knew at this point in his life that he had to do something to secure his family's financial position. He approached the situation at full speed, as if he had everything to gain and nothing to lose. His wheels started rapidly turning as he tried to figure out a way to come up with this money. Of course the streets came to mind, but he knew that he did not want to risk the possibility of losing everything he worked so hard for. One day, he walked in his bank, and his personal teller by the name of Angela was smiling at him and said, "I was just about to call you." He said, yeah right! He was feeling very stressful and I'm sure with the look on his face it wasn't hard for anyone to notice. However, the smile on her face made him feel a little funny. Angela then proceeded to tell him that his name came up on their computer system as a (5) star customer of the month. Of course he didn't fully understand what that meant, but he knew anything with (5) stars had to be good, so he had to check this out. He asked her, "What did this mean?" She said, "all kinds of doors have just opened up for you!" He said, "Like what?" She said, "do you need some money?" He said, "hell yeah!" she started laughing and said, "how much?" He said, "$30,000. She then picked up the phone and contacted a financial specialist at the bank and told the specialist that he was a (5) star customer of the month and he needed $30,000. The specialist suggested that I meet with her as soon as possible to complete the necessary paper work. He immediately left to meet with the specialist. Cat was in her office for approximately 15 minutes and came out with a closing date for two weeks for $26,000, which was cool with him! A couple of days later the specialist called and told him that she needed additional paper work. While all of this was happening, he found out he had been given a few jewels about three years prior to this time. If he had known about it, he would have been in an excellent position, as far as a paper trail. At the time, because of this lack of knowledge, he missed the opportunity to have $26,000 instead of $12,000 more. However, looking on the brighter side of things, he has $12,000 more than he had before and that to him is a good start!

Pay attention, because now I'm going to tell you what his perception of a chess game did for him. After adding up "momma's" income tax, the money from the insurance claim, and $4,000 barrowed from his mother-in-law, they had close to $30,000. Now instead of just buying the building, he had to try and "kill two birds with one stone," and put himself in great danger of loosing everything once again because of someone else. He figured if he finished the work on his house then refinanced, he could extract more money out it. By the time he had his game figured out in his mind, he will have approximately $70,000 with more equity in the new building. He then put everything down on paper and gave the proposal to his crooked real estate broker. Once he looked over Cat's paper his jaw hit the floor and he asked him, "who helped you put this together?" He said, "nobody," He looked at him in total disbelief as if he was thinking he couldn't possibly be smart enough to put together this clever financial plan without any help. He laughed on his way out of his office. Now he had another move to make in the very near future, after finishing the work that he wanted done at this time on his house.

Cat found out just recently that a friend of his he had grown up with and also purchased three of his cars from, was now involved n the mortgage business. He was already in contact with a mortgage broker who happened to be new in the mortgage game. He was supposed to walk away with some cash, but quite frankly, he really didn't feel confident that this guy could handle it. So he started on his house, or should I say he finished what he promised his wife he would finish within a year. Cat will admit, it was more than what he expected it to be., but he preserved and got it done! The equity value exceeded the amount he had originally anticipated. When it was time to make the next move, he spent damn near all the loot! But he had no problem with it, because he really believed in his plan. He just knew that if his people would just play their positions, the game that he had planned and set up would go perfectly, and he would be in excellent shape. He met with his broker and told him that he needed to make one more move. He wanted to refinance and pay off all of his loans and walk away with $25,000. Well, just to let you know that sometimes things don't always work out the way you plan. When they started everything was okay. Now remember I told you that his broker was a "slickster." All of a sudden they were faced with a number of problems, or at least that is what the "slickster" wanted them to believe. And he also wanted them to believe that he is the man who always pulls the deal off at the last minute. At the closing table, "momma" had a lot of questions, that were making Cat very upset because he trusted this joker with his life, but "momma" didn't trust him at all. However, Cat knew that they had more business to take care of in the very near future and he didn't want to "rock the boat", but there was something really slithery about this "cat," and "momma" knew it. He knew it too, but he never thought he would "snake" him. After giving everything some thought he remembered ignoring some very clear signals that indicated shadiness on this guy's part, which could later cost him everything. He held them up for 3 ½ months past their scheduled closing date, and money was very tight and he and "momma" were scheduled to go on vacation. In the meantime, their "patient seller" was gradually becoming impatient. Cat's money wasn't the way he wanted it, or should I say, planned it to be, but he and "momma" still had a good time. At that very point in time he was so stressed out that he just had to get away and relax and clear his head because he and his wife had both been through a lot! After arriving home from the falls, it was back to work as usual and more "bullshit" from his mortgage broker. There was always a lot of "built up hype" from this dude. After going to the bank to check on his credit line, because he knew he had a fresh $12,000 there, he was told by this young lady that his credit line was paid off and closed out. He was made aware that his check in the amount of $25,000 that he was supposed to have received from closing, turned out to be only $15,000 instead. He was truly upset! After thoroughly going over all the details with his financial specialist, she ran everything through again and instead of the $12,000 he was looking for, his line of credit was increased to $25,000. The next mission was to close on the building, which to him should be a "cut and dry" deal. But like I said, things don't always work out the way we plan them. Roughly (1) week before Easter of last year, it was time for Cat to restock his cloths that he sells from his barbershop business. He always tried to stay ahead and prepared for the rush of people running around at the last minute, waiting impatiently for their cuts. Then there are those people who are in a hurry to get to the mall before it closes, to buy that new outfit for Great Adventure, Wildwood, Hershey Park or wherever. So as he's always thinking ahead of the game spent an extra $2,000 on stock. He went to the shop to take inventory and the street in front of the shop was completely torn up. It looked like a war zone. His stomach dropped as he approached a police officer that was on the street, and asked him what was going on? He said the streets were being renovated and new water lines, gas lines, and curbs were being replaced. He then asked how long this was going to take place, he replied 3-4 months. Cat couldn't believe it! He knew right then and there his money was definitely going to be affected, and it was a good thing they were making moves with the real estate broker during the time frame that they were, because things really got hectic. Without any warning, it seemed as if his whole life was changing once again. And I think just one year prior, he wondered how they would make it if his income was ever affected, then pow! – here it is. Every business on the block was affected in a major way. Traffic was completely blocked off. No one could get to any stores in this section, and a lot of the store owners suffered. Some of the store owners couldn't stay open and as a result they lost their cars and homes and unfortunately no funds were set aside to compensate for these losses. But I know for a fact that the project planners were not affected at all when it comes to their paychecks. Now if this wasn't a pure case on injustice, I don't know what is. But once again, Cat couldn't let that stop what he had to do. In the meantime, he started strategically planning his marketing strategy for his book. He called a literacy agent and he gave him the total run around, and then asked him what makes him think someone would read a book about his life. He said, "Man you don't have a clue, and you will be sorry you didn't help me." Then when he did the math, Cat was glad that he faded him off, and forced him to self publish the book. So this became one of the biggest projects of his life, and he was ready for the challenge. He knew he had to train twice as hard to stay focused, and continue to be relentless in his pursuit. All the while, day after day, his real estate broker was still giving him the "run around" as Cat played his little game as he tried to be cool about it. But the more he prolonged this deal the more angry he became. Months were going by and there was almost no money coming from the shop, as he paid monthly bills with investment money and his wife Tara's paycheck. Everything was cool until his money started getting lower and lower. Every time he said something to this joker about the closing, he always had this stupid laugh and silly grin on his face as he would assure him that everything is going to be fine. He would always try and use the word "we" in order to make him feel that he was part of the team, but his trust in him was going out the window very quickly. Then the people at the mortgage company kept asking, "did you close that deal yet? – what's the problem?" He knew right then and there, his man had other motives. At this point, Cat felt that this cat was trying to wait until his cash was depleted, so he wouldn't have enough money to close on the building, because he had some big investors fro New York who were buying anything and everything they could. Now his play was for his own gain and to get brownie points with his big investors. What Cat figured was that his plan was to buy the building from the lady for cash, then sell it to him for a $25,000 profit. But the deal was a private sale, because the building was never on the market, and his mother worked for Mrs. Molock as well as his aunt Cynthia for over 25 years. She didn't want anyone else but him to have this building. He was assuming that this woman was desperate and just wanted out. Wrong, oh was he so wrong. He also didn't know that she had a lawyer representing her. He found out at the closing table when he got caught trying to do some fraud, then it was cover his track time now. He could care less if Cat got this property or not, as long as his name was clear. He was already approved for the loan with one bank. When he has seen his true colors come out, this was the last straw for him. While he was on the phone one day, Cat walked into his office while he was laughing and talking to one of his buddies on the phone as he asked if they wanted to buy this building or what? As he looked up and noticed him standing there in his office, he turned as whit as a sheet. Then he quickly replied, "Let me call you back, he just walked in." Meantime the person on the other end must have said, "Who just walked in?" He quickly replied, "Sean," as he was in a hurry to hang up the phone. Cat asked him, "What was that all about?" He replied, "oh um, I'm just trying to get this deal done for you." He then replied, "I don't know what kind of game you call yourself playing, but you are really starting to piss me off!" He then asked him why couldn't he just take the paper work back to the mortgage company that has already approved him? His response was, "we can't go through them, because they will know that we did something wrong." Cat then said, "they will know that you did something wrong, not me!" A week earlier he called his man T-bone, and ran everything down to him, and asked him if he could get the deal done in a week, he said yes. So the next day, Cat went to obtain his file from the bad guy, and he wasn't there. However, there was a brother in the office, so he pulled him to the side, told him what was going on, and asked him to get his file out of "money's" desk. He said he didn't know what was going on, and he did not want to get involved in it. He said, "I'd rather you go in his desk than me, but I need my file right now. So Cat called this joker on his cell phone and he replied with a chuckle in his voice, while sitting in a meeting with his buddies in New York, "Sean, let me call you tomorrow" He then said, "no, you don't have to call me tomorrow, I am at your office right now picking up my file." He then replied in a nervous voice, "wait a minute Sean, what are you doing he asked?" Cat said, "I'm tired of playing games with you, and I got somebody else to do this deal." He exploded, "bullshit!" – tell me what's going on Sean? I want to know what's going on! He calmly said, "nothing, I just want my file." "Listen, he said, I promise I will give you the whole file tomorrow." "Please! – just wait until tomorrow." He said, "No" "I need it right now!" He said, "Why right now Sean, what's the deal, be honest with me?" He said, "I am being honest with you, just like you've been with me." Then the nervous voice said, "Please just give me that much respect to give you the file myself." He said, "Alright money, I'll see you in the morning." The next day when Cat got to his office, he made him copies of almost everything. You can almost be sure he had to destroy the incriminating papers. Then he had all kinds of questions to ask Cat such as, "Who's doing the deal for you?" "Where are they taking it?" "If they needed any help just call, and tell them the only place they can't go to is such and such." Sean then took the paperwork to his man T-bone and told him he had already been approved at such and such bank, so take it right back to them.

When the crook found out what he had done, he was hotter than fish grease. He didn't want him to go back to that bank, because the paperwork done the right way would look different from the paper work he first prepared. Well, Cat knew that man was looking out for his own interests, so he had to look out for his. During all of this "bullshit," Sean had started working on other projects. So he had to go to the county clerks office and file his trade names, then go to the social security office to obtain a tax identification number, then back to his bank to open an account. This had to be done for everything to be decent and in order, and also to take full advantage of all the opportunities his bank had to offer.

The next thing he did was to purchase his own Internet business to advertise all of his products on-line worldwide! This business also provides him with a credit card machine and up dates all of his merchandise sold. This feature helps his accountants with their jobs. Now, Cat put in a lot of time as well as a lot of thought into all of this, but the devil just kept putting different obstacles in his way. It would have been really easy for him to just thrown in the towel, but he was determined to complete what he had started. His very next project was to buy a barbershop from a guy he knew for a long time, but the apartment building was his true foundation and had to be done first. Now during all of this time, his base income was unjustly cut-off by the remodeling of their street, but he couldn't let that stop him, he knew he had to do something. There comes a time in everyone's life where you have to make a choice to either sink or swim, and he chose to swim!

In the beginning of August, 2001, He attended a Black Writers Conference Alliance that completely blew him away! In the next month, He finally closed on the building. In February, 202, He moved into his new shop, and came out with a clothing line named "second Chance, Inspirational wear" and they are now working on a comedy video. Cat has so much more to tell his youth, but he had to save some information for another book, so be on the look out!

For all my "lil" brothers and sisters who might have started off the way he did, I tried to show you what the outcome can be. For the ones who went to prison, I tried to show you the type of things you will have to do to make it in this society today, along with a lot of prayer. So to the people who look at others and say their life is over, or they feel they will never amount to anything, shame on you! – And I say you are wrong! Where there is a life there is hope, and my God can do anything!

As For My Trial

A trial is supposed to be based on facts only! The only fact was that I was a young black man accused of a crime, and who unfortunately, had problems in the past. That was the only true fact of the entire case, with God as my witness. There was no physical evidence whatsoever, None! For this type of outcome to come to pass so easily, It is very scary for our young black men.

Little brothers, Please listen to me, "watch very careful the positions you put yourselves in, and the very company you keep, By doing so, you just may be saving your life as well as your soul."

To all the people who thought this was funny or a joke, "don't laugh too hard, this can very easily happen to you or someone close to you!"

My Letter To The Backslider

I often sit back and analyze my life, my strong points as well as my week points. I look back on my spiritual life to see where I fell and how I got in a backslidden state. When I came home from prison, I was on the right track with goals in mind.

There were several people who let me know they thought I should be doing more than I was, constantly telling me the Bible said this and the Bible said that. I already knew what the Bible said, they just didn't understand what I was going through in my everyday walk. Sometimes I ask myself, "why go through all this and still suffer?" It just seemed as though everything I went through was for nothing. That's just how the devil wanted me to feel. I lost focus and began looking back to the world and actually thought I was missing something. I took my armor off and became defenseless, which left me outside of God's grace and an open target for an attack from the devil. During this time I witnessed a lot of death. One night I almost got shot coming out of the side door of a bar. The bullet was meant for someone else. On another occasion I had four or five too many and was on my way home from a club and fell asleep at the wheel. Then there was the time when an out of town driver almost took me out when he made an illegal turn while I was riding my motorcycle.

I believe if i would have left here while in the state i was in, I would have gone to hell. A backslider who knows the truth of Jesus and knows they're not living right, lives in fear. It is not a pleasant experience, and I would wish it on anyone. The very ones that you waddle with in the mud, are the very ones that will dog you when you're trying to clean yourself up. Once you fall, the strong holds grab you and it becomes that much harder to get back. I'm writing to warn you of the dangers out there in this nasty world of ours. Stay in the House of the Lord where you are safe.

To my youth in the church, please do not succumb to peer pressure and the curiosity of your minds. Wait on the Lord and let him teach you the true and correct way to go. Always think before you make a decision or open your mouth, because you are accountable for every idle word that you speak. Trust me when I tell you that it is dangerous in the world but safety is in the church. I know quite a few people who have done the things I've done, but they did not get a "Second Chance."

I was deeply hurt by some church folk when I went to

prison, thinking there was no love in the church. This called me to look back at the world, only to find out that was in vain. Evaluating the last five and a half years, since I've been home from prison, I came to realize that the help I need can only come from my Lord and savior Jesus Christ. The road you travel as a backslider is long and hard. I've witnessed both sides, and I'd rather be on the Lord's side. I'm asking all you prayer warriors to please prayer for me. Don't judge me because like I said, sometimes man judges wrong. Only Almighty God can judge me rightly, only he knows my heart.

Never Judge A Book
(by it's cover)

By looking at a person, or their material, is unfair to label, stereo type or slander that individual, without knowing anything about them. You owe it to yourself to investigate and find out all the facts before rendering an unbiased decision concerning a person, before you decide to pass judgment. You owe it to the book, or the person, to find out the contents, as well as the character of the person, or the book, before you judge justly!!!

No excuses

In my life, I've encountered false paternity, false imprisonment; I've been set up by so called friends as well as police officers. Nevertheless, I shall scream JUSTICE, with my last breath. I've even been stabbed for trying to be a father to my daughters; I ask, "why me?" Still, I refuse to give up.

If any of these things have ever happened to you, or to someone you know, "be encouraged and know that you're not the only one with such bad experiences, and also know that you can make it."

A very wise woman once said, "if it cost you your life, it didn't cost you anything!"

Special Thanks To:

Editors: Artist
P. Timberlake Lamar Smith
S. Griffin
B. Davis
Asst. Editors: Secretaries
C. Nurse P. Timberlake
N. Austin C. Nurse
T. Timberlake

A very special thank you to the entire staff of the Black Writers Conference Alliance. The seminar was out of this world. I really learned a great deal in such a short time frame, inspiring me to pursue my dreams in writing and other endeavors, so be on the look out...

I could never forget my friend and Bro. Brian Edgeson. Thank you for all of the advice, support and direction you have given me. Best wishes with your career.

And to all of my hometown supporters; you know who you are. Thank you so much for all your love and support, which really means so much to me. I wish there were words that could make you understand how much you have inspired me to keep on trying to fulfill my goals and the ultimate, attempting to show the youth in the Pleasantville area that no matter what, they can make it happen. My message I'm sending out is, "you don't have to risk your life or freedom to have what you desire, just use your head."

The Prodical Son

The Prodical Son is a story in the Bible about a rich family who had a son who one day decided he no longer wanted to wait for his inheritance. His father, who didn't argue with his decision, gave him his portion of the family's wealth. The Bible states that he wasted his portion on riotous living until it was all gone, and the young Hebrew was forced to eat with pigs, Can you imagine how degrading that must have been!

One day when the Prodical Son came to his senses, so to speak, he realized that his father hired help who lived better than he was now living; So he decided to humble himself and go back and ask his father for work. When his daddy saw him from afar off, he was so excited, ran to greet his son, cleaned him up and had a feast, "a real party!"

Now I will explain why I felt like the Prodical Son. After suffering like a dog in the prison system, standing like a firm bold soldier for the Lord Jesus, who is the Christ, I really expected my church family to welcome me home, just as the Prodical Son in the Bible. Understand, since I was on the other side of the fence, meaning a drug dealer, I knew how those boys are welcomed home. They have a party, and I mean PARTY, they're taken out shopping for whatever they have a need of, and then they're given money and drugs, and plenty of it.

I didn't want any of the above, however, since my life was threatened for my stand as well as speaking the truth, I did expect to be welcomed home like the "true wounded soldier." After all the broken promises, the studying in school, avoiding numerous temptations and many other difficulties, I grew up very bitter because I felt I wasn't treated fairly, once again. I lost focus, just like the Prodical Son.

Through all this, God has shown me that in order to be forgiven, I must first forgive. So, to all the people who have ever done any injustice to me, I have shown them forgiveness, and now I am telling them publicly for the world to know. I forgive you. You know who you are, no names are necessary. Sorry gossipers, I'm making my way back home. I pray my family will accept me back, just please, "don't judge me, let God be my judge."

Thank you...

To My Offenders

I just want the world to know that I hold no ill feelings toward anyone who has done me wrong or unjustly. I understand! The devil provoked you.

I've learned over the years to forgive. I'm working on learning how to forget. It's not easy. I try very hard not to hold grudges, but at the same time, if I ever wronged you, in your eyes, please forgive me, and lets start over. You know who you are, we don't have to mention one name. If you don't know who you are, I'll tell you, "if you feel like someone just kicked you in the stomach real hard, or like someone just cut you, then you fit the description, but we're still cool!"

It was worth the wait

I had quite a few people who were waiting and anticipating the release of my book. In the process of preparing this project, I received the biggest and best surprise I could receive.

My wife and I were expecting a baby, in which I wanted to know, girl or boy, but momma didn't. I tried to bribe the doctor and technician who performed the ultrasound; no dice. It was so important to me and my wife for us to have a baby girl. On may 16, 2002, God blessed us with a beautiful little angel sent straight from heaven; a 7lb.9oz baby girl, Talia Olivia, and for that, I am very grateful!!!

Special Memories

Always remembering Andre Corbit for his heroic act in saving two girls from drowning, and in the process loosing his own life. A message to those two little girls is to realize that "Hype" lost his life so they could live, and to do the very best they can with their lives.

Also remembering the victims of the triple homicide on Absecon Blvd, in Atlantic City, NJ, and also the double homicide at the Homestead Motel in Pleasantville, NJ

These young brothers are gone, but they will never be forgotten!!

Conclusion

In conclusion, if you happen to have gotten lost, or decided to skip over a particular section, to wrap everything up in a nutshell; I had numerous, unfortunate circumstances to happen to me in my lifetime, and I'm sure I have some things yet to experience. It always seemed as though the odds, as well as the deck, was stacked against me. I've been lied on, falsely accused, misread, underestimated and judged wrongly. But in spite of all the all of the bullshit, I managed to educate myself in prison and be smart enough to do things the right way, through trial and error. I remained patient and persistent, making numerous investments, along with the, "I will never give up," mind frame.

I found out how to start my own family company, which is the mother of quite a few businesses. I adopted the logic, "It's not Julio, it's who you know; and if you know the right people, you can get anything done. Please believe it! " Good money management, a good budget and a bullet proof plan, can take you where you need or want to go.

Now there is a whole lot more I would like to say, but there is a certain "somebody" that is so concerned with my life, with what I am doing and what I have, that it is unreal!! I mean, their ears are kept close to the streets, "straight ear hustling," even with a couple of spies, always trying to get in my pockets.

Knowing this person is out to hurt me, hoping,

plotting and waiting for my downfall, I know I must be very careful. The sad thing is, I don't bother nobody. I'm just a young brother trying to do his thing.

So for my supporters, I send much love once again, and to you haters, I wont waste my breath or my ink, you're not worth my time. But know this, I will not be hindered and I will not loose.

BABY MOMMA DRAMA
"Walking out of the door as a Black Man"

Fella's around the world, we have camera footage of brothers being pulled from cars at gunpoint and damn near beat to death for a routine traffic stop. In another state, a brother was beat to death, tied to the back of a pick up truck and dragged for miles; in Virginia, a young black man was beat and hung with a belt, which was made to look like a suicide; in California a young brother stopped at a gas station with his father after a fishing trip, and was violently attacked after being hand cuffed by a white officer. But wait, there's more, black officers just stood there and watched; in Detroit a black man holding a rake was gunned down in his own driveway on some "Mafia-Type" shit by Detroit's finest; another brother in New York was shot 43 times and he didn't even have an ink pen to write down names.

Everyday, countless young brothers across the United States are falsely accused of crimes and sent to prison unjustly. On top of that, somebody has played us out and has us killing each other at a rate unheard of in American History. Not one of these dudes expected any of these interruptions to come into their lives, but what was mentioned was just some of the things that can hit us from out of nowhere.

And the kicker is; now we have to watch out for Baby Momma Drama. I'm writing this book as a voice for all Men who don't deserve the bullshit.

We have enough to deal with in everyday life; we do not need extra drama!

CHAPTER ONE

IT BEGINS!

The sun was shinning through the blinds of the window, Randy opened his eyes and everything was a blur. It took about thirty seconds for him to get his focus; he was still tipsy from last night. This cat's head felt like it was about to crack wide open. Between him and his boys, there was a lot of drinking and releasing going on the night before. When this joker tried to remember the events of the previous evening, he drew a blank. On top of all of the liquor that was consumed on the prior night, and from the looks of his penthouse apartment, there was a lot of liquor. This cat had problems on top of problems.

While sitting on the side of his bed, the phone rang. He answered it with a very raspy voice, "Yeah".

"Well, I see you are still alive, and that is no way to answer the phone pal", the voice on the other end sarcastically said.

"Yeah. Who the hell is this?" Randy demanded to know.

"It's me, Cuz. Harry!"

"Awe man. Why are you calling me this early in the morning?"

"Early in the morning?" Harry shouted. "It is 4:30 in the afternoon and that is exactly what I was talking about. You are taking this whole situation way too hard."

Randy asked, "Why do you always try to sugarcoat

things, and try to use fancy words to water down the truth of the matter. Man, you act like you are scared to say what it really is. Call it what it really is. Say it Harry! Say, baby momma drama. You don't want to identify or label the situation, as you call it, because your girl is about to drop that baby and you know your turn is coming real soon, whether or not you want to admit it."

Harry tried to explain that his girl is not like everybody else. Randy started laughing so hard that he almost choked.

"I would like to know what you find hilarious pal," said the voice on the other end.

Still laughing, Randy asked, "Doesn't you girl have two legs, two arms, hands, feet, a big mouth, and an attitude, just like every other normal woman?"

"Well, yeah," Harry answered with an uneasy tone.

"So. What makes her so different?"

"Well. It is just that she does not act like the rest of ya'lls girls. And, she doesn't treat me the way ya'lls girls treat ya'll.

Randy exploded, "That's because you are still with her, and she didn't have the baby yet. But the day is coming buddy, and I can't wait until you finally get to see just what the rest of the fellows and I have been talking about and going through. Then I want to see just how calm and understanding you are my man!" CLICK! "Hello? Hello?"

Randy sat there with the dumbest look in the world on his face, like he could not believe Harry just hung up on him. Not less than twenty seconds later, Randy's phone rang again. "Don't you ever let up?" Randy screamed into the phone.

Then a nasty voice came through the line, "No, I don't and I won't for the next 14 years. Is my check in the mail?"

Randy realized it was Cindy on the phone, therefore,

before he said anything, he tried to calm down so an argument wouldn't break out, especially since he had not seen his son in over three months. "Yes. The money for the support order is in the mail. I don't know why you didn't receive it yet; I mailed it four days ago. But while we're talking about court orders, you have not been obeying the visitation part."

Cindy said, "And I'm not going to either. And if I don't get my money today, you're getting locked up – and by the way, your son needs new sneakers," CLICK!

Randy was not surprised at all at the reaction Cindy displayed regarding his statement. Ever since they broke up, she had made it her point to make his life a living hell. She did everything from harassing him on his job to playing on his phone; anything she could think of to spite him, she would do it, no matter what the cost. Even though Randy truly knew this, his only concern was being a part of his son's life.

While sitting there pondering over his and Cindy's entire relationship, it hit him how quickly they went from being so much in love, to becoming enemies. He also thought about why he was being treated so grimy even though he was the one trying to keep the peace. He does not want his son exposed to that type of environment; you know, watching his mother and father argue all the time and never able to have a civil conversation. But he knew how heartless, selfish, and cold his baby's momma could really be. The phone rang; it was his cuz, Harry again. Harry was trying to tell his cousin about a therapist who specialized in "baby momma drama".

"What? A therapist? So now you think I'm crazy, huh Harry? No. I won't go see any therapists about nothing," Randy shouted into the phone with a look on his face like he could kill the world.

Harry said, "I'm only trying to help you, Cuz."

"If you want to help me, mind your own business when it comes to something you know absolutely nothing about. You don't know or understand just how vicious or evil this woman truly is. She is full of poison with her conversations, as well as her actions. But you don't see all that Cuz, so I understand that you can't see the seriousness of this whole thing. I apologize for what I said on the phone earlier. It was the truth, but I hope you don't have to go through this type of bullshit after your babies are born. I wouldn't wish this on my worst enemy because I know the only one who is going to suffer long-term is my son and there is nothing I can do about it."

Randy said, "Look cousin. You woman treats you the way she does because ya'll are still together. But I promise you that if you ever leave her, you will see just what I mean. Cindy crossed me, ruined our entire relationship, and now she is very jealous because I'm prospering in life and I have a new love. So, she thinks she can hurt me by using my son by any means necessary".

CHAPTER TWO

ANOTHER CHARGE

Later on that evening, while riding down the highway, one of Randy's partners hit him on his cell phone. The name registered on the phone as soon as it rang, so Randy knew who it was.

"What's up slick Willie?"

"Slick Willie ain't slick Willie today yo!"

Randy replied, "What the hell are you talking about Ray?"

"You ain't gonna believe this yo!"

"Talk to me li'l bra. You don't sound right."

"Man, I didn't want to tell you, but I know I need your advice for real now, Baby Boy."

Randy demanded, "What happened?"

"I got locked up last night-"

"You got what?"

"Hold up Randy, that's not it. My peoples came down to bail me out and a warrant for child support came up that I didn't know anything about."

Randy interrupted angrily, "That shit don't sound right."

"Yo Bra, the warrant was for thirteen thousand, cash, on top of the ten grand for the bail bondsman."

"Bail bondsman?" Randy said.

"Yeah man!" Ray said with a very depressed and disappointed voice.

Randy figured out very quickly that his childhood friend was in some serious trouble. If he had to pay ten grand to the bail bondsman, this meant his bail was one hundred thousand cash because you only pay ten percent. So, he knew the charge was serious, but since Ray did not say anything about the charge, and only mentioned the warrant for child support, he asked him only about that. Randy learned at a very young age not to pry into other people's business when they do not want you there. After paying bail, Ray found out that the mother of his children went and filed for child support. While there, she told the people that he hasn't paid her any money in six years. "So that is where the thirteen grand came from," Randy said with a voice of disgust.

Ray said, "Man, you now better than that. I give that bitch anywhere from three hundred to five hundred a week. Yo bra, word is- I feel like-"

"Ahh!" Randy shouted. "Don't even say it bra! Trust me when I tell you, I know how you feel. I tried to tell you a long time ago to stop giving that broad cash. I told you money orders! That way you have proof that you have been giving her money. I hate to say it, but she's going to get that bull shit off. I know you don't want to hear it, but it is the truth. Listen bra, I'm going through some serious shit too with my baby momma. She is on some real live shit, yo! But I don't even want to tell you about my problems right now with the shit you goin' through, but if you need someone to talk to, I'll be here."

Ray exploded, "What the hell did you think I called you for, fool!"

Randy started laughing, "I don't think we should talk about this on the phone, so let's set up a li'l get together for tomorrow night. Are you free?"

"I am now, after posting $23,000 for bail," Ray said sarcastically. "And the part that makes me sick is, I know all that money is gone. I can't get it back and it's still not over."

Randy asked Ray, "Are you all right, Bra? You sound like you're ready to cry."

"Man, you must be out of your rabbit, ass mind. I'm straight gangster!" Ray replied.

"Yeah, I know. That is exactly why you're in the position you're in now."

Ray said, "What the fuck do you mean by that?"

"Calm down partner. I'm only telling you the truth. If you weren't out doing gangster shit, you wouldn't have gotten locked up."

Ray responded by saying, "I know you are telling me the truth, but right now I don't want to hear that truth."

"Okay, so I'll tell you what you want to hear," Randy said. "Don't worry about anything, you are going to get all of your money back, and the case you caught is going to be dismissed."

"Ha, Ha. Very fucking funny," Ray said. "Why do you have to be a wise ass all the time? I thought you would be the one in my corner, Dog."

"Listen Ray, you know I'm down with you. I just don't want you walking into something blind, and not looking at the reality of the whole situation. But trust me when I tell you, I know how you feel. Like I said, I'm going through it with my BM (Baby Momma) too."

Ray chuckled a little bit and said, "Randy, they don't play fair man. She went down there and lied on me number one, but I think she set me up, too."

"What the hell are you talking about, Ray?"

"I really don't want to talk about it on the phone, I'll tell you when we link up. I'm out, yo. I gotta go lay down, I feel sick to my stomach."

"Yeah Bra. I know that feeling. And, that is the best thing you can do, and try to eat something, One."

CLICK!

After hanging up with Ray, a million thoughts crossed Randy's mind; now, not only his Baby's Momma Drama, but also exactly how the "Law" might look at his and Ray's relationship. Ray didn't want to talk on the phone, and he knew what kind of business his childhood friend was involved in. Ray was one on the biggest drug dealers in South Jersey. And while thinking about his friend's line of work, he remembered saying "What's up partner" on the phone once, but he knew that there were no business ties what-so-ever, of any kind.

Ray, on the other hand, couldn't eat or rest at all. Every time he thought of what just happened, and imagined what type of legal issues lie before him, and the very thought that this whole ordeal had just cost him almost thirty thousand, and it's just beginning, his blood boiled. Just knowing that his "BM" was partially responsible, if not totally, had his nerves so screwed up the man didn't know if he was coming or going. He jumped on the phone immediately. The phone rang four times, she must have looked at the caller identification before answering with a sarcastic laugh, "I see you still had enough money to make bail, huh!"

"Jackie, why like this? And why are you always worried about how much money I have? It ain't none of your business how much paper I have. I take damn good care of you and my kids. What would posses you to go to the pigs on me, and then tell lies on top of that?"

"Jackie responded in the coldest, nastiest voice you could imagine, "What the hell would posses you to go out and buy your li'l tramp a brand new car, and a four-carat diamond ring?"

"Oh, so that is what all this shit it about, my fiancé!"

"Fiancé!," Jackie screamed at the top of her lungs. "I know that is not what you just said!"

"Yeah. That's exactly what I said."

"Ray, how are you going to marry that-"

"Don't even try it," Ray cut her off before she could finish, "At least I know that she, unlike you, really loves me and cares about me. But not you, all you're concerned with is how much money I got, and how much I'm going to give you. But I should have known better from the jump. You ain't nothing but a gold-digging whore, and you're going to pay for what you just did to me."

"Oh, are you threatening me, Ray?"

"Call it what you want," CLICK. Ray said what he really felt. He really couldn't believe Jackie would do something like this to him after all he did for her. He paid the mortgage on the house, and gave her at least $300.00 a week for her and the kids. Even though they weren't together, Jackie was still trying to control Ray in her own little way. And when she realized that she was only playing herself out, she started getting nasty, threatening him with child support and talking about his drug deals. If she ever caught him with another woman, he would always laugh and say, "Yeah, whatever. Just keep playing your position and you'll be all right." She would always reply, "Think I'm playin' if you want to".

Deep down inside, and all things real, she knew Ray was seeing a couple very beautiful, and elegant young ladies, who were not only gorgeous, but also college graduates. So, that also had her feeling some kind of way. And it just so happened that a rumor got to Jackie that Ray was expecting a baby by some new chic he just met. Jackie got word eight days before Ray was arrested.

Ray was trying his hardest to believe that Jackie wasn't the cause of this, but the reality of her threats haunted him like a living nightmare. All that rang in his ears were her bone chilling threats, which made him sick to his stomach every time. It would pass though his ear. "Child support and Police...Child Support and Police...Child Support and Police...Think I'm playin' you if you want to". Now he knows for sure that she wasn't playing.

The more he thought about it, the hotter he became. He jumped up and raced across town to Jackie's house. When he put the key in the door and realized that she changed the lock, this cat's blood pressure shot to the moon. He straight lost it right there on the front porch. He started beating, kicking and screaming at the front door, "Bitch. I'm going to kill you when I get in this door." The next-door neighbor called 911 and so did Jackie.

Because of the double call, seven units responded to the scene, and Jackie truly played her part, crying to the police saying she was in fear for her life. Ray was arrested again right there on the spot. The police asked Jackie if she wanted to press charges. She said, "Yes", looked Ray right in his eyes and said, "I also want to sign a restraining order because my neighbor and I heard him say he was going to kill me." Ray's heart shattered into a thousand pieces. And she had the nerve to sit with this devilish grin on her face as if to say, "I told you what I would do". Ray was now charged with domestic violence, terroristic threats, and harassment; along with all the other charges from the past. Bail was set at $100,000 cash; no bail bondsman. After all of the money he just put out for the initial charges, Ray knew this was a major set back. He only had one phone call at the police station, and he only had one person he knew he could count on. When Randy's phone started ringing, the name on his cell phone came up *Pleasantville Police Department,* and Randy almost shit on himself. The first thing that popped into his mind was that somehow the police got his number from watching Ray. He took a deep breath to get himself together before answering.

"Hello," he answered with a somewhat frightened voice.

"Yo Ray, thank God it is you. What are you doing calling me from the police department?"

"It's a long story, but that bitch Jackie called the pigs on me again and chumped up some more charges."

"What do you mean more?"

"Just what the fuck I said. She had something to do with the original charges. But listen, they're holding me on $100,000 cash bail."

Randy said quickly, "I don't have-".

Before he could finish talking, Ray cut him off, "No, man. I need you to contact my mother and let her know where I am, and I need her to go get the money and take it to my lawyer and let him bail me out. That way they won't ask her any questions about the money, and he'll know his retainer is already paid. And, tell him to put this on the top of his priority list. Make sure you say thank you. I'm sure he won't have a problem after he gets that cash."

Randy's mind was going in a totally different direction from his childhood friend's. Randy truly believed his money could solve all problems. Randy couldn't turn his back on his friend, but did not want to jeopardize his freedom either. So he told Ray it wouldn't be a problem, but he really wanted to see him A.S.A.R.

Ray said, "Now I heard of A.S.A.P., but what's the R for?"

"Release money, and I mean as soon as-"

The officer said, "Okay. Time is up."

Ray replied in a low tone of voice, "Alright player, you got that."

As soon as he hung up the phone, Randy's head felt like it was going to explode and he started feeling sick to his stomach. The joker found it was becoming hard to breath and then he started sweating. He jumped up and ran to the bathroom when his mouth started getting watery. As soon as he lifted the toilet seat, it was like a faucet was turned on. This lasted for a good three minutes. After washing up and getting himself together, he looked in the mirror and could not believe his nerves were shook up like that over a phone call. He couldn't, or didn't want to imagine those silver bracelets around his wrist. To be real, this Cat was scared to death of any kind of incarceration. He's never been in any kind of trouble, let alone in a situation like this. Randy's nerves were shot, his stomach was all in knots and he kept feeling like he was going to vomit.

After drinking a couple glasses of water, his stomach seemed to settle and his mind started racing 100 miles per hour. All kinds of crazy, paranoid thoughts were running through his mind.

He really didn't want to get involved, but his close friend was depending on him. So, he made the call that was asked of him. Ray's mother could not believe the words that came through the phone to her. She shouted, "That stinkin' Bitch!". Randy couldn't believe she said it. Ms. Edna never took a liken' to Jackie, from the first day she met her, but she knew that it was impossible to choose her son's girlfriends. Ms. Edna was from the old school, you know, kind of old-fashioned. She didn't like the ways of the so called 'new millennium woman'. She thought they were too fast, and too loose, if you know what I mean. Jackie's image, attitude, and mouth didn't help her with Ms. Edna at all. Deep down inside, Ms. Edna believed that one of the kids was not her grandchild. Ms. Edna knew her son wasn't an angel, and on an unconscious level, she knew of her son's street dealings. She also knew her son was paying for Jackie's lavish lifestyle, which Jackie didn't mind living at all. She knew Jackie had it in her from the evil look Jackie always had In her eyes, and she also knew Jackie was only in it with her son for the money. She also knew that one day Jackie would do something to hurt her son, she just did not know exactly what this female would do. After hearing all Randy had to say, Ms. Edna just sat on the phone crying, "What next? I don't think I can take much more of this…this boy of mine. And his drama with this girl is going to be the death of me."

"Oh no, please don't say that Ms. Edna, it's not that bad!"

"It's bad enough baby, but this isn't your problem. I'm so glad my son has a friend like you. I'll call the lawyer right now. You know," Ms. Edna said, "I don't blame everything on this li'l nasty girl. They say an apple doesn't fall far from the tree, and I met her nasty-as mother. She was so nasty lookin' and triflin' that Blind-Eyed Jimmy could see where that li'l hooker got her training, or lack thereof. I'm so sorry about my language, but Ms. Edna is a little upset baby! I'll talk to you later, Sugar. Bye-Bye."

Ms. Edna cried out to God as she was hanging up the phone, "Lord, please forgive me for cursing. I know you said be angry, but sin not. It's just… I don't know what this son of mine is going to get himself into next. God, I don't know how much more this heart of mine can take. Lord, only you can give me the strength to make it through this. God, change his heart so he will do right. I did the best I could to raise that boy up right, but ever since his daddy died, he's just been out of control, no matter what I do. God, I just want him to do right."

She attempted to regain her composure while praying and dialing the number. Just as she was clearing her throat, the voice of a happy, little, white girl said, "Hello. Victor Jones…Attorney-at-Law…how may I help you?"

"My name is Edna Robinson. I'm calling to speak to

Mr. Jones about my son, Ray!"

The secretary responded, "I'm so sorry, but Mr. Jones is in a meeting right now. Please call back", CLICK!

Ms. Edna said to herself, "I'm about to lose my religion again. That little bitch didn't just hang up on me, No… no…! I'm not calling right back, that isn't anything but the devil trying to get me upset and kill me." What Ms. Edna didn't know was Mr. Jones's meeting was between his secretary's legs having a little something to eat. That's why she was so short.

Ms. Edna went to stand up and holding her chest, fell right back down in the seat, "Oh God, please help me." She staggered to her room, laid down because she was feeling dizzy, reached over and grabbed the phone, dialed 911, dropped the phone on the floor and passed out. The operator was saying, "911, may I help you? 911, may I help you? What is your emergency?" After the third question the operator knew something was wrong. While looking at the computer to get the address from where the call was made, she sent the police, ambulance, and fire companies on high alert.

Within minutes, sirens where blazing all over town. Everyone knew the address was Ray's Momma's house and they knew her son did a lot of dirt, but his mother was an angel. The police arrived first, and not knowing what to expect they kicked the door down with guns drawn. After entering the house, they secured the scene and found Ms. Edna lying on the floor by the phone. "Medic! In here quickly," the sergeant on the scene yelled. When the emergency team ran in the room, the Sergeant asked who the supervisor was. A little short, white dude that looked like Poign Dexter jumped up and said, "Me, Sir".

"Listen to me and you listen good son, I don't care what you have to do, but you help her with everything you know. This is a great woman!" Then the sergeant called the situation in to the station to say that he had everything under control. After giving orders to his officers, Sergeant Gram made his way back to the station to tell Ray himself. You see, the sergeant use to coach Ray in various sports with the P.A.L. organization. He kept a close eye on Ray over the years, and he knew what role Ray played in the streets.

He never tried to put Ray in any compromising position, but he did let Ray know that if he ever caught him doing wrong, he would do his job. But the relationship with Ms. Edna was different. Sgt. Gram had the highest respect for Ms. Edna. He knew she was a single mother who tried with every ounce of strength her body could muster up, to bring her only child up the right way. She worked hard, and never used the welfare system, or asked anybody for anything. She was a lady with a lot of class and a lot of pride. He also knew how much Ray and his mother loved each other. Because of Ray's reputation on the streets, some officers wouldn't be too sympathetic to the problem at hand, and for that reason, he decided he wanted to tell Ray himself, face-to-face.

Meanwhile, at the attorney's office, Mr. Jones was busy pulling up his zipper, his secretary was wiping her face, and the telephone was ringing. Knees still shaking from just getting his socks blown off, old boy caught himself cracking a joke, talking about, and "Saved by the bell Huh baby?"

She just smiled, thinking to herself, *Yeah, saved from the three-inch killer.* Her thoughts made her laugh harder than his joke, but his dumb-ass just thought he hit a home run with that one because she was laughing her ass off. She kept thinking, *A three-inch, two minute killer!* The very thought was very hilarious to her.

The answering machine finally picked up with the

company message of being out to lunch. Randy could not believe it, he didn't even want to leave a message. Maybe Ray's momma already called him. Little did he know, right about now, Ray should be the last thing on his mind. Contemplating whether or not to go to the station house, his telephone rang, "Hello," Randy answered.

"Yes. This is Sgt. Gram from the police department. I'm calling for your cousin Ray. Something is going on concerning his mother. He asked me to call you so you can check on her at the hospital."

"Okay. Tell him I'm on my way there!"

"I'll relay the message," Sgt. Gram said.

Randy had a thousand thoughts running through his mind as he ran out the door. While driving, he called Ray's lawyer again from his cell phone. The answering machine came on again. Randy snapped o the phone, "Listen you cock-sucker! This is the third or fourth time I called you today! My cousin Ray is locked up and he needs you right now! I know for a fact he has done a lot of business with you! Don't do him dirty now! His mother is in the hospital and he needs to get out of jail!" CLICK.

Randy then called his own mother to tell her about Ms. Edna. That was like putting it on the local news, being that Randy's mom was the president of the city's gossip club. Within one-half hour the news was all over town. There were so many different stories, ranging from falling in the bathroom to falling down the steps, to what ever you can think of. Randy couldn't do anything but pray for Ms. Edna and ask God to touch the hands, hearts, and minds of Ms. Edna's Caretakers and doctors.

Very concerned with the well being of his aunt, Randy left his car in the emergency lane, ran to the front desk, and asked where they took Ms. Edna. The woman at the desk asked Randy for his name, identification, and relationship to the patient. Randy was very angry and demanded to know the status of his aunt.

Sitting in the stinkin' cell, unattached to reality because of the news he just received, Ray's patience grew shorter and shorter by the second. Very upset with the fact that he was completely helpless at this point, and for the first time in his life he found himself completely out of control when it came to his emotions.

As he sat quietly crying on the bed, he remembered something his mother instilled in him since he was a child, "When ever you come across a problem too big for you to handle yourself, do not be a fool, cry out to God! He'll hear you if you are sincere in your heart".

It has been a long time since Ray took some time to acknowledge God, but his momma didn't raise no fool, and it is always better late than never. As he began to try to talk to God, he unselfishly begged the Lord to help his mother, not him. His words were real and straight from the heart. He first acknowledged all the wrong that he has done and how he wished he could switch places with his mother.

Meanwhile, down at the attorney's office, Mr. Jones sat relaxed and feeling good after that serious lickin' his secretary gave him a few hours ago. He was on the phone with one of his golf buddies – another crooked ass lawyer named Billford Harris. He was the lowest of low; the kind of lawyer who will sell you a dream, take your money, then sell you down the river and keep the same shit eating grin on his face the whole time he's fucking you outta your money and your freedom.

He's definitely one of those lawyers who have a lot of political pull. You know, he and the prosecutor have lunch and discuss how much money is involved with the case. In other words, he wants to know how much his cut is and he reminds his partner not to forget the break down with the judge if he wants it to go a certain way. Yeah, that is exactly how it goes down.

Billford had to cut the conversation short because he had to call his bail bondsman (BB) to go get one of his clients. That's when Mr. Jones remembered Ray.

So, he called his B.B. as well and told him when he gets some free time to go pick up Ray from the police station, and to make sure he gets him before they send him to the county. If they take him to the county the process will be much loner. Although he could give two shits about Ray personally, 'financially', Ray was a good guy 'to his pocket', that is.

Back at the police station almost immediately after Ray couldn't pray anymore, an officer appeared with words like an angel, "Time to go home Mr. Jackson." It took every bit of energy and strength Ray had inside to hold those tears of joy back; but it was totally impossible for Ray to hide his appreciation to God for answering his prayer. Ray clutched his fist very tightly, raised his arms to the heavens while slowly bending his head back, and expressed his thanks to God. Ray was so happy he completely forgot how mad he was at his slimy-ass lawyer for taking so long to come get him.

Chapter three

RAY'S DAY IN COURT

Finally walking up to prepare for his day in court from a somewhat restless sleep, Ray's telephone rang. He looked at the caller I.D. and was slick to his stomach when he saw his BM's (Baby's Momma's) name come up. A million thoughts quickly ran through his head, and the first thing he thought of was, *This bitch go to be out of her mother fuckin' mind thinking we have anything to talk about after all the bullshit she just came at me with.* Then he said out loud, "I don't feel like arguing with you right now, bitch. I'll see you in court." Then Ray's answering machine picked up the call and he couldn't believe this chic was trying to be nice on court day. But he knew from previous experiences that she was slithery like a snake and could never be trusted. He knew she was just that vicious and unpredictable.

So, he continued to get dressed while listening to the bullshit message, and then he heard something she said. Money thought to himself, "I know this Bitch ain't reading me no poem on my answering machine".

Jackie's voice could be heard clearly reading,

"The Man I've Been Searching For"

The man I've been searching for already knows what
    it means to be a real man.
He's not too macho, and yet he's not too soft.
He's rough around the edges, but with the gentle
    spirit of a newborn baby.
The man I've been searching for doesn't need to be
    taught how to treat a woman.
He knows all the right things to say and do, and he
    knows about all the warm and soft spots of a
    woman's body too.
The man I've been searching for isn't afraid to
    express his feelings to me.
He's the kind of man who knows that expressing his
    pain isn't a sign of weakness.
He's knows he's never less than a man even if he has
    to shed a tear.
The man I've been searching for is a king in every
    aspect of the word.
He's definitely strength and sensitivity wrapped into
    one.
He's my king and the one man I've been searching
    for."

After reading this poem, Jackie hung up the phone
without another word.

About two hours later, while waiting in the lobby at
court, Ray still had a really sick feeling in his stomach.
Then her nasty-ass come over with her oldest daughter's
clothes on and enough make-up to paint a clown. She
looked like a straight whore. Ray thought about how
embarrassed he was to tell anyone that he had kids by
this broad. She was like a teacher with no students, "No
class".

Ray just sat there shaking his head as if to say, how
could I get myself caught up with a nasty bitch like this?

He couldn't believe Jackie would go out like this: *lies, set-ups; really trying with everything she could think of to knock him off board and land him in jail, by any means necessary.*

While sitting in the courtroom waiting to be heard by the so called "honorable Judge;' Ray got a chance to hear some problems that other men from all walks of life were going through.

Ray saw a lot of injustice being done in and out of the courtroom. Ray looked into the face of some of these men, studied their actions and their body movements. He knew from seeing this that these men were neither acting out a lie, nor telling a lie. He could see the pain and anger all over each man's entire being. And, in every case, it seemed like the Judge Actually hated every man that stood in front of him. The Judge would cut them off while they were speaking, tell them that they are liars and that he doesn't believe anything that they are saying. He took sides with every woman who was in the courtroom, and ended every case with an increase for the bitch and a two-miss stipulation policy, which would disperse an automatic bench warrant if two payments were missed. So, knowing what was about to go down when his name was called, Ray started daydreaming.

He was so tired from the damn-near sleepless night before. The sleeplessness started from Ray trying to pinpoint where he and Jackie's problems first started. All he could remember was the hot sex and the way this chic used to suck his dick. Still daydreaming, he realized that the great strain this broad used to cause this cat was the exact start of all the bullshit; not to mention his mom being sick.

Ray thought to himself, "Ain't this a bitch. This slick-ass bitch played me from the beginning. She got off on head, worked the old boy over, blew my socks off, and then played me out". Felling like a straight sucker for so-called 'love', he realized this bitch had been playing him out from the very beginning.

One thing Ray finally realized was if you let your dick do the thinking, it could cause you a lot of problems and aggravation, and cost you a lot of money. All he could think about was how much time and effort he put into this weak-ass relationship, which finally ended up here, in front of fake-ass kangaroo court, with no justice at all in sight for anyone.

Then he turned and looked at this evil-ass bitch he had to deal with and Ray got sick to his stomach. He threw up all over the courtroom, all over everything, and ran out the door to the bathroom, still giving it up.

Jackie couldn't believe what she just witnessed. That dumb-ass bitch felt all embarrassed because she knew it was her face that made Ray call 'uncle earl'. The Judge called recess to have the courtroom cleaned up. Ray returned to the courtroom in about ten minutes after cleaning himself up in the bathroom.

The sheriff at the door saw what happened and knew Ray didn't have a toothbrush in his pocket to tighten up his breath after that embarrassing incident. So, he found himself trying to offer Ray one of those powerful mints, called Altoids. If you know anything about Altoids, you know they are the truth for a nigga with bad breath.

Ray was very offended by the gesture from the officer, so he glared at him and said very quickly and sharply, "What you tryin' to say, you eatin' mother fucker!" The sheriff couldn't believe that this joker just screamed at him after he was only trying to be courteous. But, being in the court room on a regular basis and knowing what eventually happens to these cats before they leave, Sheriff Gray didn't want to make a scene. Even though he was an authority and could do this ignorant-ass nigga real dirty, he knew the judge was about to knock his boots loose.

Plus, ain't no sense in the judge being mad at him for disrupting his courtroom.

The sheriff looked at Ray and said, "We will see who laughs last before you leave this court room today, my man. Now sit your punk-ass down before I lock your simple-ass up chump…I mean, champ."

Ray started to respond, and then thought better of it. He knew he had enough problems as it was now, so he did just what he was ordered to do. Right as he was about to take his seat, the judge walked in. You know what happens, someone says, "All rise…", and then he allows you to be seated.

Ray looked at the expression on the Judge's face as soon as he walked back in and could tell this mother fucker had an attitude before he heard anything form anybody. Ray looked over at his triflin'-ass B.M. and almost gave it up again. "Call the next case in." the Judge demanded.

As roll call continued, the court clerk started yelling Ray's name, and he was automatically in motion toward the front of the courtroom. When the Judge saw who it was that was up next, he made a joke, "She really makes you sick, huh? Ray just looked at him and made the best decision at the time, which was to keep his mouth shut. It almost killed him to hold his tongue, but he knew he didn't have all the power he was accustomed to having.

Ray now sat next to a dude in the courtroom who noticed Ray's movements and the expression on his face. This guy caught himself giving Ray some consoling words. He asked Ray a question, "How many times did she call you in?"

Ray answered very aggressively, "This is the first time. Why?"

"One kid or more?" the guy asked

Ray turned and looked at this kid and the expression

on Ray's face said he really didn't want to be bothered right now, but reluctantly said, "Two."

The man made the dumbest remark at the wrong time. This fool came out of his mind and said, "Well, you better get use to it 'cause these broads are like vampires searching for blood, and their baby daddy is usually their victim, especially if you leave their dumb-asses. That's their only way to try to hurt you."

Ray exploded, "Why don't you shut the fuck up! If I want your advice, I'll beat it out of you. So mind your fuckin' business."

The guy tried to apologize. Again, Ray just looked at him and said, "Yo, kid. You don't know me B, and we are going to keep it that way. Got it! Now beat your feet, son." The dude just rolled his eyes like a little bitch.

Ray sat in the courtroom, listening to all the bullshit these brothers had to go through and how the judge sided with the women in every case he heard. Ray couldn't believe how hard the judge was on the fellas. Stevie Wonder could see the bullshit these chicken-heads were coming into the courtroom with, and the judge just let them get it off.

Some of these sticky-ass hoes didn't even work. They have three baby daddy's paying child support, a nice welfare check, section eight, food stamps, and their mother, brothers, and sisters living in the same house, and they still come to court for increases. And once again, they know the judge is on their team, so they end up getting what ever they ask for.

Ray sat there and thought about all of the bullshit he's been hearing all day, and came to the conclusion that this whole situation with this court was set up to completely divide the father from their children, give control to the broad and to extort the father. So Ray knew he was in a fucked-up, no-win situation, and for the judge to be acting like this toward every male that stood before him, meant this mother fucker must be gay. Ray busted out laughing and everyone in the courtroom turned and looked at him, even the judge. Things returned serious very quickly. The look the judge gave him took all the humor out of his thoughts immediately. Ray knew there were only a few cases left and then he would have to stand in front of this faggot-ass peckerwood. Ray's thoughts had him chuckling again. Ray knew this time he fucked up because the judge asked him if he wanted to share the joke with everyone so they could all laugh together.

The temptation was so great, and since he was on a roll with his humorous thoughts, while looking at the Judge he blurted out, "I don't think everyone would think it is funny your Honor."

The judge replied, "You're a real live-wire, huh. We'll see how funny you are in one minute." Ray knew he fucked up for real now. One more case left and the judge is shooting him rocks. Ray's leg started jumping and he started to perspire profusely. Then he got little butterflies in his stomach. So, he thought about everything and said to himself, "fuck it. He's going to do what he wants anyway, so ain't no sense in being shook now. I'm going to curse both of these motherfuckers out today. The whole time, this bitch Jackie was sitting there with a smirk on her face, applauding every case the judge ruled on, knowing this situation was going to go in her favor". Ray thought, *I wish I never met her.* Then he thought about how many times his mother told him that the tramp was low-down and no good. Ray thought his mother was a little old-school and she just didn't like her, but what he failed to realize was his mother was always a good woman and after seeing the evil in Jackie's eyes from day one, and after meeting Jackie's mother, and seeing what trained her. Ms. Edna knew the broad was nothing but trouble.

Shaking his head in disgust, Ray continuously thought of his mother's words and her present condition, which only added fuel to his own fire. Looking at Jackie's facial expressions and examining her past track record of action and sincerity, he knew for sure that poem she read on his answering machine was 100% pure bull-shit.

"Nope", Ray thought, "I will not fall for the banana in the tail pipe."

The next case to be heard was the last before Ray had to face the judge. Ray sat in court for a couple hours witnessing the slaughter of men before him, but this last case was the worst of them all. He thought Jackie was bad. Oh my God, this chicken was unbelievable. This dude, Charles, was calm and very soft-spoken. I guess from previous court appearances, he knew what ever he had to say wouldn't mater one bit, so he opted not to speak at all. The judge was very familiar with this clucker because of her very heavy file case. This broad had six kids by five different men. However, Charles was the only one who she consistently kept in court, viciously trying to suck every dollar she could possibly get; sort of like a vampire drains a body for blood until every drop is gone. She used each and every tactic available to her, especially the one provided by the system. Ray came to find out that this broad was back in court for an increase again, after she just sparked him up about seven months earlier for damn near a mortgage payment. But she saw Charles in a brand new car and almost lost her mother fuckin' mind, especially since her little 'hoopty' was broken down and Charles knew it. There was nothing he could do.

The judge giggled and said, "Okay Ms. Anderson. What is it this time? Why are you asking for an increase?"

In the most ghetto way ever spoken, this bitch said, "Just because I want one."

The judge replied, "didn't you just get an increase a

169

couple of months ago?"

Ms. Anderson replied, "Yeah. But I heard he got another job and a new car."

It fucked Ray up to hear the judge's reaction. "Ms. Anderson, you just received an increase a few months ago. So I'm rejecting your request for another increase and just because the man has a new car doesn't mean you get an increase." Then he asked Charles if he had anything to say.

Charles answered in a soft-spoken tone, "Your Honor, I've been going through pure hell for no reason at all, literally, since I met this young lady. This woman has children from three other guys beside myself, but I'm the only one who pays child support, and I don't feel that I should be the only one paying. Basically, she uses my money to take care of all of her kids, and whoever else lives with her. Then, anytime she feels like she wants a couple extra dollars, except for today, you give it to her. We have a visitation order that she totally ignores. I complained about it in the past and nothing was ever done. This stinkin' bitch-"

"Hey!" the judge yelled.

"I'm sorry, Your Honor," Charles said. "I just get very upset when I start talking about this whole matter. She calls down to child support every week, precisely at the deadline to see if I paid. She does this because you put a two-week stipulation on me and she can't wait for me to be late or miss. She would love nothing more than to have me locked up. And to tell you the truth, I might have seen my son for five or ten minutes, maybe eight times in the past year. I can only see him at her house, on her terms, and sometimes she will not even let him answer the door.

The truth being told in court was killing this bitch and she didn't get what she wanted. The fact that the cat

170

was out of the bag in public and she was being exposed for the gold-diggin' whore she really was made Charles' blood boil.

She blurted out, "That's a mother fuckin' lie" But no one believed her. She didn't even believe herself. Nobody wants to look in that mirror.

The judge checked her quickly. "That language will not be tolerated in my court room. And, one more outburst like that and I will hold you in contempt of court. Do I make myself clear, Ms. Anderson?"

"Whatever!" was her sarcastic reply.

"What did you just say, Ms. Anderson?"

"I heard you!"

"Do you see what I mean Your Honor? She can't take the truth, and when you don't do what she wants, there's a problem, which could always turn into something serious. That is why I'm always here. It is not because I don't care or that I'm a dead-beat daddy. It is because I chose to have a baby with a monster," commented Charles.

"Okay, Okay. No name calling," interrupted the judge.

"Your Honor, this woman has been extorting me for years and using the court system to do it."

The judge looked at his watch and decided this was going too far. The whole time this was going on, Ray's mind was racing. *Damn, that's the second case I heard that was not that bad. Maybe I should keep my cool.* But he knew he fucked up with the jokes early in the game.

Listening to what the judge was talking about took Ray back to a previous case in a flash. This was the only other case that the judge was halfway decent with. It was a reduction case that some guy from prison put in because he just came home. It seemed as if he was in the rears because they were charging him "street child-support" on an inmate's monthly income. Rumor is, every prisoner that comes home tries to get this adjustment and they never get it. Ray overheard this dude, Kevin's brother; tell him he was wasting his time. He was all hyped up, talking to Kevin, yelling and screaming.

Kevin said in a low voice, "During your case, did you talk to the judge the way you're talking to me right now? 'Cause if you did, I can see why you didn't get a reduction." The problem was the Kevin's child support was $65 a week, according to his income prior to incarceration. So, while he was gone and couldn't pay the money, it just mounted up. The judge had the usual, 'like I give a fuck' face on until Kevin explained himself. The judge was impressed with Kevin's over-all appearance, personality, and choice of words in describing his situation and how he felt. Kevin explained to the judge that because of his unfortunate prison experience, due to circumstances beyond his control, he was $13,500 in the rears. He explained that upon incarceration, his income drastically change from $400 a week to $30 a month. So, if child support is based on a person's income, when his income changed, so to should have his child support payments. Trying to get $65 a week from $30 a month is like trying to get blood from a rock and everyone knew that couldn't happen.

To everyone's surprise, the judge said, "You're right."

Kevin's B.M. flipped out right there in the court room, "What? What do you mean he's right? I had to take care of the kids by myself, the whole time he was in jail."

The judge said, "Number one, you better get yourself under control in my court room, young lady. Number two, you are lying to me because looking at your file, and Welfare has been supporting you since you started having children. Number three, this is my court room and what I say, goes, and don't you ever forge that." The judge calculated the time that Kevin was locked up, made the adjustment, and called the next case.

Upon returning his thoughts to the present case, Ray thought, *maybe the judge is not that bad.*

The judge told Charles, "Although you have a legitimate argument, I cannot rule on it because that matter was not filed with the clerk. After you file, we will listen to the whole case in its entirety. But, if you do not make a motion, it cannot be heard." So, he was told to file a ProSe_Motion correctly, then his side of the story could be heard. "Case dismissed!"

Ray looked around and he and Jackie were the only two left. He started getting butterflies in his stomach at first, and then when he looked at his B.M., the butterflies turned to rage. "What the fuck are you smiling at, Bitch!" Ray snapped.

"I suggest you get yourself under control, Mister. This is my court room, and you will not disrespect my girls in here," said the Judge.

CHAPTER FOUR

DOES HE WIN?

"**A**w, Shit!" Ray thought to himself, "this bitch got the upper hand already; 'she's his girl." Ray knew right then and there that he better play it real cool.

"Let's start with you," he said to Jackie. "Why are we here today?"

"I came here to get child support and file a restraining order."

"How many children are involved?"

Jackie answered, "Two."

The judge turned his gaze to Ray, "Why have you not been taking care of your children, Mr. Jackson?"

Ray almost blacked out right then and there, but thought about it for a minute, caught his breath, and answered, "I give the Bi..., woman, $250.00 to $350.00 a week your Honor."

"That's a lie!" Jackie blurted out.

The judge said, "All right, that's it. You two will not use my courtroom for a shouting match. I'm a judge, not a referee. Neither one of you is to open your mouth while the other is talking. Do I make myself clear?" Neither said anything. "Continue on, Mr. Jackson."

Ray felt a little more comfortable after the Judge checked this broad. Ray continued, "I run a dating service, and some times of the year are better than other, but I always make sure my kids have what they need. She is mad because I do not give her everything she wants. Ever since we broke up and I gave my new girlfriend an engagement ring, Jackie has been acting real shitty. She gets upset because I will not respond to her weak attempts of seduction. I really don't pay her any mind because her only concern is what I'm doing with my life and my new love. Therefore, she concocted a story full of lies to give you and the police. Why, because no one really wants her. Please get her off my back."

The judge asked Jackie, "And what do you have to say?"

"Number one, he don't have no dating service. He's a half-assed pimp and a drug dealer." Ray could not believe this bitch just said that. His blood started boiling and he was glad he did not fall for that bullshit poem read on the phone earlier that morning. He looked at Jackie with a look of pure disgust, but he kept his mouth shut. "And, he don't give me no money. And don't nobody give a fuck about his little bitch!" You could see the fire in Jackie's eyes as she began to hyperventilate while speaking. You could look at her and tell she did not believe what she was saying herself. Anyone could see the jealousy and envy in her eyes as she spoke.

Ray just sat quietly, thinking to himself, *After all the help I gave this chick, she would do some bullshit like this.* Although she had no proof at all of these accusations, she attempted to put the spotlight on Ray with attention that he didn't want or need right now. He knew from that point on that his BM was now in the top five on his enemy list. No way could he ever trust her with anything.

The judge's words interrupted Ray's thoughts, "Mr. Jackson, do you have anything else you want to add?"

Ray sat quietly for a minute; just thinking how it would be a real pity for him to bring up how trifling this hoe is and how her whole family has been sponging off the welfare system for the past twenty-five years. This was a family tradition passed down from Grandma. Ray decided to remain silent and just shook his head, no.

The judge looked at Jackie and said, "Since you said

he has not been paying you, I'm going to put a judgment in for #150 a week."

That bitch screamed, "WHAT?" The judge told her to shut her mouth while he is speaking and to never interrupt him while he is speaking again. 'Billie Bad-Ass' was crazy, but her dumb ass wasn't stupid. She just sat there looking like shit.

On the other hand, Ray couldn't believe the judge took his current situation into consideration. And oh was he glad. He looked over at Jackie with a half-assed grin and it was like throwing gas on a roaring blaze. She shouted out, "What the fuck you laughing at?

The judge ordered the sheriff to lock her up immediately for contempt and he set her bail at $10,000. Ray was like, *oh shit!* He was that surprised, but he didn't feel sorry for her. After what she did to him he could care less what happened to her now. He thought, *that bitch got just what she deserved. My mother always said, 'What goes around comes around sooner or later'."*

As she was led out in handcuffs and crying, the judge said to Jackie that he will make sure she gets a copy of the complete order since she has to leave. Everyone giggled out loud. Ray could tell she was very embarrassed and felt like shit. But that is what she gets for trying to be greedy and spiteful.

After the rest of the instructions, court was dismissed. Ray still couldn't believe how shit just went down, especially after his courtroom behavior. He knew he had to bounce to the hospital to check on his mom, but he knew he still had a lot of mess to straighten out. After a few minutes, he started feeling kind of sorry for his BM and he couldn't understand why. This broad tried to ruin him and didn't care one bit about it. But he knew why, after thinking about it. He felt bad because of the big difference in the way they were brought up. A real woman raised him and she was raised by...well... what ever you want to call her mother. He felt bad for her, but no way would he do anything to help her.

He couldn't help but thing about all the help he tried to give her, in spite of everything she put him through, then his mind started racing. *I gave that bitch everything she asked for except to live with her in a world of bullshit. She called the police on me on numerous occasions; she was so possessive and insecure; she always felt guilty about her little secrets; she would accuse me of doing what I fond out she was guilty of; she would physically attack me every time I left the house; she destroyed my clothes and tried to alter my image in the streets. Then I found out that the li'l girl she said was mine was not and she knew it all along. She tried to trap me and thought the whole time that the bullshit was going to work. I over looked all of that bullshit through the years, and still tried to be civil with this bitch, even though we weren't together for the kids' sake. Then, after I left her dumb ass, she started hounding me for money and tried to destroy my relationship that I was involved in. Now she's lying and trying to extort me through court litigations. And I have the nerve to feel bad now. Aw, hell no. Fuck that stinkin'- ass bitch. She deserves everything she gets. I have no love for her and never will again.*

CHAPTER FIVE

I LOVE YOU, MOMMA!

Ray had to catch himself because just the thought of how Jackie crossed him made his blood boil. He knew he was the last father in the world that deserved some bullshit like this, and he had more important things that needed his attention; like his mother and the rest of those chumped-up charges that his chicken-head momma put on him.

When Ray walked into the hospital he saw a young cat from the neighborhood arguing with a young lady about the results from a blood test he just picked up. Ray got sick to his stomach when his mind went back to the day he opened up that letter. On that day, his eyes scanned through the pages looking for two words, "final results". Ray's memory was oh too clear; like he just opened the letter all over again. Ray tried to hold back, but couldn't stop a few tears from escaping from his eyes. Make no mistake about it, the tears were not for Ray, they were for the little man. Ray knew what the li'l brother was going through. He wanted to stop and say something, but he knew the time was not right for either of them. Shorty needed time to heal, and Ray needed to see his mother.

This was Ray's first time seeing his mom. When Ray walked into the room and saw all those I.V.s and tubes attached to his mom, all the gangster flew out the window; Ray broke down and cried like a baby. He just sobbed and mumbled over and over again, "I love you, Momma. Please wake up!." As he sat there, many childhood thoughts ran through his mind; events that happened in his life that made him and Ms. Edna's relationship so close. Ray's thoughts were interrupted when the doctor walked in the room.

"Hi. How are you doing? I'm Doctor Adams. You must be Ray."

Ray did not like doctors at all because he thought they were arrogant; at least all the ones he knew. So, he answered sharply. "Yeah. What's going on with my mother?"

"It seems as though your mother suffered a slight heart attack. This could have been caused by stress and anxiety. In the midst of that, she somehow lost consciousness and maybe hit her head from falling down. She was fading in and out on us upon arrival. But, yesterday around 6:30 pm, after we stabilized her, it seems as if she slipped into a comma. Now, her current status is serious but stable, and we have been keeping a close eye on her. We believe her body shut down because of her blood pressure, so right now we are happy that things are stable. However, you can trust and believe that we are doing everything we can for her. It seems as though she is a very important lady because she must have had 150 to 200 visitors already."

Ray looked at the doctor and saw the sincerity in his eyes, then stroked his mother's hair back and said, "She is the best mother in the world and the greatest woman alive. Can't nobody say nothing bad about my mother, and she is all I really got."

The doctor looked over, and from looking at the heart touching scene of a grown man crying and holding his lifeless mother who's being kept alive by machines, and could not fight back the tears. Dr. Adams quickly caught himself and told Ray that he would call him and keep him up dated on everything.

As Dr. Adams walked out of the door, Ray shouted, "Good or bad, Doc, I want to know". Ray didn't know which hurt more, the fact that there is a possibility his mom could did, or the fact that he can't get any advice from his confidant and true friend. So, he tried to figure out just what his momma would say in this situation.

He thought about all the times he talked to her about problems he often encountered with Jackie. And believe me, it was often. Ray tried to pinpoint exactly when and what went wrong.

He tried to weigh the good times to the bad times. The bad time side was definitely winning the sea-saw, if you know what I mean. The good memories were few and far between. Ray actually pulled out a paper to write it down so he could really see it for what it really was. He remembered when they first looked cute together, then they started dressing alike; you know, the same clothes matching every day. They always had fun at the movies, walks in the park, music by the ocean, weekly outings to dinner and the clubs, and all the hot romantic scenes you could ever think of. And trust me, this bitch, Jackie, was a real freak and she wanted to hook Ray bad.

The problems started when Jackie's mom got involved in their relationship. Her mom told her to fuck the shit out of Ray real good, at least two or three times a day. She told her to, "Lick his ass and suck his dick and balls real good. That's how you turn a nigga out on the pussy, baby. That's right, feed him, fuck him and put his ass to sleep. That's how you trap a mother fucker".

Ray found out the exact words of the conversation from Jackie's mom and from Jackie's Aunt Gloria. Gloria felt bad knowing all along that they were trying to trap Ray. Although, she felt like she could not betray her niece and her sister. But when she found out that Jackie fucked her boyfriend, not only did she tell Ray what went down, she gave him some pussy too. Ray laughed when he thought about that then, and he laughed even harder now because the bitch Jackie, didn't know that Ray fucked the shit out of her Aunt Gloria; they kept that between them.

Ray remembered very quickly why he left. Ray couldn't go anywhere while he was with Jackie. That Bitch was s jealous that when he came in the door from a trip to the corner store, she would accuse him of everything in the book. She was a very evil bitch, but she had a side a nigga could love. She did things sexual to a nigga that were unreal. All Ray could do was shake his head and think, *I don't care how bad a bitch is or how hard the pussy snaps, it ain't worth all this bull-shit. And if any of this plays a part in my Momma's condition, I'm going to kill that stickin' bitch.*

Ray remembered his mother's first words to him after meeting Jackie for the first time, "She is not for you son. She looks sneaky." But Ray did not listen. Boy did he regret not paying heed to his mother's words. Ray thought that when Jackie first tried the oky doc with the first kid she said was his, Momma didn't even have to pick the baby up; as soon as she looked at the little boy, Ms. Edna said, "That ain't no grandson of mine." That is when Jackie began having a problem with Ms. Edna. Jackie had a problem with her because Ms. Edna knew and called the truth as it was. Jackie was mad because she couldn't pull the wool over Ms. Edna's eyes, so she stayed as far away from Ms. Edna as possible. And the farther the distance she put between them, the more her dumb ass confirmed Ms. Edna's gut feeling that she was a true snake in its very essence.

Ray thought about all the deep conversations he had with his mother, things he wouldn't talk to anybody about because he was trying to protect his real feelings of how scared he was for his children being raised by such a vicious person like Jackie. The reason the fear was so great was because he truly saw for himself the old saying, "The apple don't fall far from the tree." Ray didn't want his child brought up like Jackie was, but what other way does she know then what she was taught. "And people wonder why we live in a fucked-up world", he said out loud.

Ray remembered telling his mom how Jackie was controlling the children's minds. How she wouldn't let him spend time with his children alone and about all the lies she would tell the kids to manipulate their minds into believing anything and everything she said. She would tell them that their father didn't love them and how he was trying to take them away from her. Ray told his mom that the only time Jackie would let the kids call was if they wanted something, and the only time they could spend the night was when she wanted to go out for a weekend fucking and sucking spree. Ray found out the events were public knowledge because the streets talk, and Jackie slept with the community. If there was any one thing Ray was ever embarrassed about, it was people knowing he had children with Jackie.

After watching her son pour his heart out, Ms. Edna could always feel Ray's pain and it would always upset her uncontrollably. But she would always try to give Ray good motherly advice. Ray could recall the most serious advice his mother ever gave him, which he was not ready to handle. Ms. Edna said, "Son. I know this is going to hurt you because I know how you love those children, but son, you have to let them go! Let them go."

"Momma, what you mean, let them go. I'll never do that, Mom. They are my kids."

Ms. Edna said, "Son, I know those two are your kids and Jackie knows you really love them. But she is playing with witchcraft and she is going to damage those kids for life, if she hasn't done it already just to hurt you, Son.

Now, I know what I'm saying is very hard to accept, but I'm telling you what's best for you and your children. I told you when I first met her li'l hot-ass that she was going to be nothing but trouble. All she ever tried to do was hold you back, and as soon as you started looking good and making your own moves, she realized her position had changed and she was on the outside looking in. She didn't like the picture you were painting because she was not in it. So, she would use anybody and everybody she could to get you off track and loose your focus. She would stop at nothing to destroy you, even if she had to use her own children. Think about it, Son. You and your girlfriend have traveled the world; not just the states, ya'll, go to other countries, and she has never been out of the state. You live in the suburbs and she lives in the projects. You bought your girlfriend a B. M. W., and she has a bus pass. Your girlfriend is draped in diamonds, and she doesn't even have a birthstone. Do you understand what I'm saying, Son? The woman is jealous and mad because she never had that with you. Now she doesn't want you to have it either! Don't worry about your children, when they get old enough to understand what she has been doing, they will understand why you did what you did. But if you keep going like this, with the fighting and carrying-on, you will be doing nothing but keeping yourself upset and in trouble."

Ray missed all of the advice from the heart that his mom use to give him. Ray didn't trust too many people since meeting Jackie, and the only person Ray could talk to about a lot of things was his mother. He couldn't believe that at one time he actually loved this bitch; but evidently, by the present actions of this whore, the feeling was not mutual.

Ray could not do anything but think about everything; all of the low-down dirty tricks this broad tried to pull and all the advice his momma use to give him because of it; all the lies she told, the bullshit letters, the sweet empty bedroom talk. He thought, "I wonder how many niggas she told the same bullshit bedroom lies?" He remembered hearing Jackie's mom talking about bills that were due, and then he remembered how many dudes she said she was going to fuck to get them paid. Ray couldn't believe she said it right in front of Jackie. As he thought about it, he shook his head and could only imagine what this bitch was teaching his daughter. The more he remembered, the sicker he felt. There were just too many bad memories and not many good ones at all. And, all he could say was, "How did I get caught up with a woman like this? The sad part is the nightmare continues day after day; if I would have just listened to my mother."

Ray looked down at his mother with tears in his eyes and said, "I love you, Momma." He sat back in the recliner and tried to relax. That is what his mom would always tell him when ever he got upset. Ray was so exhausted and stressed that he ended up passing out right then and there. While sleeping, he had a slight nightmare that he took for a sign. He had a dream that felt so real that he had to take it as a sign. It seemed like Jackie sweet-talked her way back into Ray's life using her sexual expertise and deceitful charm. Both which were passed down from her mother. It seemed like everything was smooth, then all of a sudden it seemed like a hundred faces flashed across his mind. Most he knew, yet some were so called friends that Jackie very easily serviced, one way or another. All had promised not to tell, but all had very freaky stories and experiences of their own. All of these stories and experiences had very graphic descriptions of different passions and erotic events, down to the costumes and shit she loved to perform. It was like every skeleton this bitch ever tried to hide in her closet seemed to fall out at one time, like a graveyard. All this flashed through Ray's mind like the speed of light. Then Ray saw Jackie in a cloud of smoke, dressed in all black with the most wicked laugh he had ever heard; somewhat like the devil.

He awoke drenched in sweat and went to the bathroom to wash his face. While looking in the mirror, all he could say over and over again was, "I should have listened to you Momma". Then the reality hit him; the nightmare is not over.

He was startled when he looked up and saw Harry sitting there with his mom when he walked out of the bathroom. Harry was at the hospital at least once a day. He was Ray's closet and truest friend; almost like a brother. They clapped hands and immediately embraced each other. Ray couldn't hold it any longer; he broke down in his best friend's arms. Harry was fucked up right away because he never ever saw Ray like this.

Harry tried to console Ray and told him his mother would be all right. But Ray was very upset and finally broke down and let his true feelings be expressed, and he was not trying to hear any shit. He blacked out in a rage stating, "All this is that Bitch Jackie's fault". Then he started talking real reckless and Harry knew Ray was half crazy and was capable of doing just about anything, so he tried to calm him down. After finally convincing Ray to at least hear him out without any interruptions, which was something only one other person could do, they both looked at her upon Harry's request.

Harry said, "Listen. What would your mother say to you right now?"

Ray hesitantly replied, "She would tell me to calm down and think."

Ray hesitated and again he reluctantly replied, "She would say, 'I know you don't want to hear I told you so, but I did! Now the damage has already been done and you cannot change that, so don't worry about something you cannot change, just focus on the things you can. Find a way, then do it."

Harry smiled and said with a low voice and tears in his eyes, "That's how your mother can talk to you right now. You know she would encourage you to improve your situation with every ounce of your being. You know your mom would not want you to self-destruct in any situation. She taught us better than that."

Ray swallowed all his pride and said, "You are right, Cuz. I really need to handle this differently. It is just that all of this bullshit is really unnecessary. I don't fuck with that broad like that. Why me? Her other baby daddy's give her their ass to kiss, and the bitch don't get a dime from them, nor does she fuck with them the way she comes at me. I only tried to help the dumb bitch after all she put me through."

Harry said, "Cuz, that is just how some women are. You just chose to get involved with the wrong one. Like your mom said, you can't change that, you just have to deal with it the best way you can."

"Yeah, I know. I really need to talk to my kids. I don't want them to suffer because this shit done go real ugly, and I don't know what type of poison she has been feeding them."

Harry said, "Hey, Cuz. I heard about a support group that was designed for brothers who go through all this bullshit we've been going through."

Ray started laughing at first, but when he saw how serious Harry's face was, he stopped. Ray asked, "Are you going to check it out?"

"Yeah, you want to go with me just to check it out? You never know, it might do some good."

Still undecided, Ray Said, "I don't know. Let me think

about it Harry. But I got to go take a shower and rest a little, this whole shit is too much."

"I can dig it, Bra. Call me when you wake up. The session starts at nine o'clock and I'm leaving around 8:30. I can't wait to see what this shit is about and how it's set up."

Ray looked up and said, "Yeah, you sound pretty souped up!"

The guy they told me about said that it was the best move he ever made in his life. He told me he almost killed his baby mom because of her bullshit and the dumb bitch didn't even know it. But he said the program saved his life, which in turn, saved her life. He was really glad for that, and then he started laughing and said, "That bitch ain't worth sitting in jail for". After hearing everything he had to say about the program and how his life has been since then, Harry firmly admitted, "You're dam right I'm souped. I can't wait to get there."

Ray was very impressed with the courage his friend showed in expressing his true feelings and how he was trying to improve his life. Ray told Harry to call him at 7:45 to wake him up and he would go with him. Harry was very surprised by the response from Ray, but was very glad Ray was going for two different reasons. One, because maybe this was something that could really help his friend deal with this part of the bullshit in his life, and two, so he wouldn't have to go for the first time by himself (SUCKER). Harry kissed Ms. Edna on the forehead and as he was rising, he could have sworn Ms. Edna winked her eye at him.

Startled, Harry jumped back. Ray said, "What's wrong?"

Harry didn't want to say anything to Ray because he was not sure of what he saw, so he had to think quickly. He said, "Nothing. I just want you to know you mom is going to be alright." He quickly walked towards the door, a little spooked out, and said, "I'll call you at a quarter to eight."

Ray kind of thought this cat was acting kind of suspicious, but really wasn't sure. Maybe I'm so tired that I'm delirious." Ray just shook his head to get refocused, and then looked over at his mother. A nurse walked in and it was obvious that Ray was entirely drained, emotionally, as well as physically.

The nurse said, "I know it is rough, but we will take good care of your mother. Go on home and get some rest, you look like you really need it."

Ray looked over in the mirror and could see the stress on his face. He simply agreed with the nurse, kissed his mother and told her he would be back in a couple hours.

CHAPTER SIX

WELCOME TO THE CLUB!

The drive home seemed endless to Ray. It was hard to focus on one thing in particular with everything going on at one time. He still couldn't believe all this shit was happening to him.

While sitting there pondering everything, Ray chuckled a little when a verse from a rap song came to his mind, and how portrayed role in the song mirrored his present situation. Ray thought, *and it was all-good just a week ago.* Then he mumbled, "Ain't that the truth."

Ray pulled into his driveway and noticed it was time to get his landscaping done. As he walked in the door, he quickly turned the security system off, and right then and there started stripping off his clothes and headed straight for the shower. Sweaty, grimy, hot, sticky, and exhausted, Ray climbed into the shower, placed his hands on the wall to hold himself up and just let the water rain on him. Ray never appreciated his own shower so much. To him, it was a refreshing experience, like he never had before.

While standing under the water, Ray focused his thoughts on how he could improve his current situation. The words of his mother bombarded his thoughts, 'Change what you can, don't worry about what you cannot control…just change what you can!' "Yeah, that's where I'll start." Ray said out loud, "Changing this whole problem with this bitch first." After saying that, Ray was kind of excited about the session that night. After the soothing shower, Ray grabbed the towel, stepped out of the shower, dried his face, and focused on the man in the mirror. He asked one question, "Why me?" Starring into his own eyes, Ray said, "Shake that shit off nigga. You've been in worse situations. Get yourself together and handle your business."

Ray finished drying off, brushed his teeth, put lotion on his body, threw on some silk P.J.s, and turned on the television. But before settling down to relax, he hit the button on his answering machine to check his messages.

When Ray began listening to the first message on his machine, breaking news came through the television. It was easy to tune out the answering machine when Ray heard Jackie's voice. The terrorists had just bombed a U. N. building in Iraq and blew up a bus full of Jewish worshippers in Jerusalem. The photos of the tragedy caught on tape brought tears to Ray's eyes. Just the thought of all the innocent lives lost and the news clippings of the little children slain for issues they don't even completely understand were absolutely horrific for Ray. To imagine the way of life for these people in this part of the world is almost unbelievable, if not for the news reports and the footage.

Ray thought, *and we have to go through all the bullshit just to have a relationship with our kids.* Ray found little humor in one of his thoughts. Ray said out loud, "They should charge all bitches that are guilty of this bullshit with domestic terrorism for their lack of concern for the well-being and poisoning of the minds of the children who are our future." Then a little true sarcasm from Ray, "And they wonder why the world is so fucked up today. Children are made to believe that they are not loved; they are being used like pawns in a chess game, all for the cause of parental politics. What is this world coming to?"

Ray took a deep breath as he shook his head to the reality that is often over looked or under seen, and quickly fell off to sleep.

190

Meanwhile, Jackie had been released earlier that day on her own recognizance, and was already plotting on trying to get back at Ray. See, she had to because her plans didn't go the way she figured them to go. Jackie was on the phone calling all her family members trying to get them involved with her bullshit. She told them a bunch of lies, as usual.

One of her cousins, Rahim, knew the truth and knew Ray, so he told her that she needed to stop all this nonsense and just face the fact that their relationship was over and the man didn't want her or anything to do with her. "He doesn't bother you and he isn't thinking about you; he has a girl already. He doesn't want you, get over it! And, you may not realize it until it is too late, but somebody can end up getting seriously hurt or even killed for that bullshit you are doing."

Jackie blurted out, "Aw, you are just a scared-ass pussy. But you don't have to worry about it punk, I'll get somebody else to step to his ass!"

"Naw, I'm not worried about it, and I'm not scared or a punk, I just know the truth. And the truth is that nobody in our family needs to go to prison or get killed over your lies, 'cause when the smoke clears, you don't and won't give a fuck about us after you use us. Anyway, that is exactly why Ray don't fuck with you now, you evil li'l bitch!"

Jackie couldn't take the truth Rahim was telling her, so she hung up on him.

In the meantime, Harry was finally starting to see a little of what the 'boyz' mean. His little girl is an infant, and post-partum is busting his BMs ass; all she has been doing for the past few days is bitching, complaining, and nit-picking about everything. He called Randy to tell him what has been going on and Randy laughed and said,

"Not Mr. 'My girl is not like you guys' girls'. I told you, I told you, I told you! There is going to be something that she is going to do that is going to piss you the fuck off; my advice to you is don't let her know it is like that. Oh my God, she'll never stop. As a matter of fact, she will apply pressure by the day, until you feel like you are going to lose your mother fuckin' mind. Well my man, the only thing I can say to your rookie-ass is, Welcome to the Club!"

CHAPTER SEVEN

SESSION ONE

"Well, I don't know about it being exactly that serious, maybe I might be jumping the gun a little," Harry said in a very nervous voice. "Who are you trying to convince with that bullshit right there?"

Randy said in a sharp and intimidating voice, "You or me?"

Silence fell for forty-five seconds, and then Randy started laughing and said, "It's just getting started, Money. You ain't seen nothing yet; but I know you don't want to hear the truth, so I'll chill. Alright?"

"Why are you so quiet? Reality is a motherfucker, ain't it. I told you, but now you don't believe shit stinks until it's sliding down your throat. Tastes nasty, don't it? I don't mean to be hard on your 'fam', but now you see why I told you long before you were talking about things you never experienced. This is what I meant. If you have never been through it, you cannot understand how something real small can become a giant instantly, and that's 'word'. I know you wish you never told me, right? Well, maybe it was the best thing you could have done, how 'bout that! You might have a big advantage we didn't have."

That comment woke Harry up a little bit, "What do you mean by that?"

Randy said, "Ray and I are going to a Baby Momma Drama session tonight. I think you should go with us so you can get some insight early in the game, Money. 'Cause word is bond, you're going to need it."

While the words were sinking in, slowly but surely, Harry thought of all the horror stories his friends and colleagues had talked about over the years, and for once, he thought, *What if it is really as bad as they say?* Then he thought about how many family members he personally bailed out of jail for child support bullshit and he said out loud, "Oh my!" with reality gripping him tightly.

Harry could not believe the way he was physically feeling about his thoughts, and the fact that his baby was not even one month old really bugged him out. He didn't want to sound as desperate for guidance as he really was, so he caught himself answering in a nonchalant way, even though his facial features expressed fear, "Yeah Randy, I think I will go check it out with you guys tonight."

Randy laughed and said, "Yeah! I bet you will. We don't sound so silly or ridiculous now, do we?"

Harry defensively asked, "Why are you laughing at me?"

Randy said, "It's just the way you say that 'you guys' shit; that fucks me up! Ever since you came home from college you sound just like a nerd. But you know we still love you Bra, so cool ya jets, Homie".

"Just because I don't use street terminology like you guys...I...I mean..."

"Let it go Harry, let it go. We're bouncing at 7:45; I'm out."

"Listen!" Harry shouted, "Before you go I have a question to ask."

"What's that?"

"How's Ray doing?"

"He's alright, considering everything that has happened over the last twelve days, but you can ask him yourself, and if it will help you to know, he's jus as excited as you."

Randy said, "Look man. I know you can sit and talk all day, but I got to roll. I'm about to go to the mall and get me some new sneaks and some new drawers."

"New drawers...for what? The meeting tonight?"

"Naw, man. Just to say I got some."

While driving to the mall, Randy's call phone rang and Cindy's name came up on the I. D. "Oh, hell no! I'm not answering the phone for this bitch to fuck my day up; because that is all she is trying to do, some how, some way. It is either that or she is trying to beg for more money. And, I know she will loose her mind if she knew I was getting some sneakers and new drawers for myself. That bitch will try to get an increase. I can't let the thought of this broad mess my day up. I'm going to get some new drawers".

Later on, Ray woke up in a cold sweat from a nightmare where Jackie invaded his dreams once again. Jackie was riding the shit out of Ray, fucking him with no sympathy, when in the dream, her eyes turned a bright yellow and her tongue was slithering just like the snake she is; always has been and always will be. Ray shook his head and knew he needed to go tonight. He actually toyed with the thought of what that pussy was like after all these years. Then the dreams and memories of all the bullshit quickly reminded him of what that poisoned pussy must be like after all these years. Then Ray thought, *I could slap myself for even thinking about that bitch after all the bullshit and after fucking all my boys like it was nothing seriously done.* Then he said, "Yeah! I know I might really need this meeting. Shit, this bitch was trying to steal my money and my dreams, literally".

Randy called Ray and Ray answered with a somewhat happy tone, "What's really good wit'cha?"

"Damb! You sound a lot better."

"Yeah, nigga. I hope I feel a whole lot better after we get to this meeting. Yo, I'll meet you down there, I'm getting dressed right now."

Before leaving the house, Ray called the hospital to

check on his mom again. The nurse at the desk answered. "I. C. U, Mrs. Randoff, how may I help you?"

"Hello. This is Ray Ja –", the nurse cut him off very quickly.

"Your mother's status is still the same, but it seems her vital signs have picked up and that is a good thing. Are you coming down now?"

"No, not just yet. I'll be there in a coupe of hours. I have some serious issues to check out first, but as soon as I'm done –"

"I know, you'll be here right away," Mrs. Randoff said in a light-hearted tone. "The women in the hospital only hope their children love them as much as you love you mother".

CHAPTER EIGHT

BACKFLASH – DOC, I DON'T KNOW WHAT TO DO.

Earlier that morning, about 9:20 am, Dr. Sampson walked out in to his lobby and saw the scroungiest man he had ever seen in his life. "Well, hello. May I help you?"

The man looked up with the saddest eyes the doctor had ever seen. The man sat there staring up in the air for a few minutes with his lip trembling. He was trying to get his thoughts and his words on the same page. When he finally tried to speak, he became all shook up and could no longer fight back the river of tears that began to flow down his face.

Dr. Sampson, in all of his years of counseling, never witnessed such a sight. It kind of scared him for a minute. For the first time in his profession, he was at a loss for words. The only thing he could say was, it will be okay; over and over again, it will be okay, just calm down. The doctor advised him that he would be right back and walked to the back room to get the man some water, a towel to wipe his face, and to turn his security cameras on. He couldn't believe that he left the door unlocked before it was time to open.

Dr. Sampson had to install security cameras because he got a few death threats from some of his client's children's mothers. They hated the fact that Dr. Sampson brought such a practice to their city. Ever since he opened seven months ago, domestic violence dropped 67% in the city. Also, 40% of all his clients were able to receive child support reductions because Doc taught them their rights according to the system. So, there were a lot of mad chickens in the area, and I mean furious. These hoes couldn't stand the fact that someone was there to show these brothers how to deal with their BM's bullshit. Doc couldn't understand the situation in the lobby, but if it was truly that bad, he wanted to help the man. Doc is a big boxing fan and believes in following instructions. The last instruction given to the fighters before engaging in combat is, "Protect yourself at all times".

As he walked back into the lobby, Dr. Sampson realized that the unknown man finally got himself together because the dude was wiping his face with his shirt, while mumbling an apology to the doctor for breaking down like that.

The doctor replied, "It is quite alright," as he thought about the heart-breaking scene of a grown man crying like that. But Doc knew for a fact that whatever it was that broke him like that was very heavy and very serious. Dr. Sampson introduced himself and asked the man what his name was.

The man slowly responded, "My name is Roger Fisher, and I'm really fucked up in the game right now, Doc. I can't take it no more and I don't know what to do. If I don't get some help and direction right now, I'm going to kill myself or somebody else, or both".

Dr. Sampson was shook now, and when Roger realized what he just said, and saw the look on the doctor's face, he quickly said, "Oh. I'm sorry Doc. That statement is not directed toward you. I over heard two brothers talking about some similar problem that I'm going through and how much you helped them. I can't lie. When I first heard about a counselor for baby momma drama I thought the whole idea was absolutely insane, until this bitch pulled her last stunt".

Dr. Sampson still didn't trust this cat because he just

looked both suicidal and homicidal, and he walked around talking recklessly. So, he knew he had to handle this situation properly to insure things wouldn't get out of hand. He told Roger that he had to fill out a registration form and asked him if he had insurance. Roger almost snapped out and broke down again, but he caught himself and said, "Doc. I don't have insurance. I don't have a job. I haven't had anything to eat in four days and I'm two days from being homeless-".

Doc cut him off as he tried to continue, "Roger. I understand you are having a really tough time right now, but these sessions cost money. How are you going to pay? This is a business and I also have bills to pay." He looked at Roger's face and watched him change expressions that went from bad to worse.

Roger said, "I understand Doc. I just needed a little help, that's all".

"Wait a minute. There are a few programs available to provide financing and insurance for you."

Roger started smiling like that was the best news he heard in a long time, but because of the Doctor's bust schedule, Roger had to come back to get the information he needed to straighten out his monetary problems. He needed to take care of that first, and then make an appointment. Roger was trying to understand, but his sad and withdrawn look told the true story. As he was turning to walk towards the door, Dr. Sampson felt very bad that he had to turn this guy away when it was too obvious that there was a grave issue that seriously needed to be addressed. Therefore, he decided to bend the company rules just a little. "Wait a minute, " said the Doc. "I'll help you out a little until you get your paperwork together, but you have to work with me. Alright?" With a very nervous voice, the doctor said, "I really don't know why I'm even doing this." The Doc continued to advise Roger, "I have an appointment in fifteen minutes, so you go take care of you paperwork at this address. This will get the process for funding started. Explain your situation and tell them I'll be working with you and they will take it from there. My last appointment is over at six o'clock tonight, make sure you are here by 6:15 pm and we will work on getting you straightened out. Here's $20, go get something to eat and get yourself a haircut and shave. And, we'll take care of your grooming later as well."

Roger couldn't stop thanking Dr. Sampson enough. The man walked out of the office with some hope that better days might come and it started with some food. Dr. Sampson saw how happy and excited Roger was. He just smiled and said; "I'll see you at 6:15."sharp.

CHAPTER NINE

BACK TO RAY

While driving to the session, listening to 50 Cent, Ray's cell rang again and Ray looked at the caller identification and saw Randy's number. "State your business," Ray answered.

"Turn the music down for a minute," it almost sounded as if this cat was crying.

"What is wrong with you, Fool?"

"Yo Bra. They just murdered li'l Johnny!'

Ray snapped, "Man, stop fuckin' playing."

"I'm dead serious!"

"Who did it?" Ray asked.

"His girl's father and brother!"

"What?"

"Yeah, man. This bitch set him up using his son. They told him that if he didn't come get him right now, he'll never see him again and that she's going to make sure of it. The nigga went to go see his son because he knew the bitch was half crazy when he met her. While he was sitting out front in the car they ambushed him and gunned him down." Silence fell across the line for a minute. "Ray," Randy called.

"I'm still here, Man. That shit just fucked me up."

Randy continued, "And I just found out the bitch called his dad and said, 'Your son is a dead man as soon as my father and brothers catch his ass'."

Ray just pulled over to the side of the road, "Ah, Randy, I'll be there in a minute." CLICK! He sat there for a few minutes thinking about how many confrontations he got in with Jackie's family and how easily he or one of Jackie's family members could have been the ones getting killed. He called Randy back immediately, "Put the word on the street to find those cowards before they get out of town."

"Too late, Homie. They are locked up and in protective custody."

"What?" Ray shouted. "Protective custody! What is a killer doing under protective custody?"

"Ray, we're supposed to be going to a meeting to prevent these problems for ourselves, right?"

Ray quickly answered, "Yeah! Yeah right. I'll see you in a minute."

After getting his mind together, it was still hard to accept the fact that he will never see li'l Bra smile again. What made it worse was the fact that these faggots murdered his little people and he can't get to them right now 'cause these faggots are in P. C.!

Ray pulled up in front of the building where the meeting was being held. Before he went in, the thought ran across his mind that Li'l John's son will never see his daddy again. Then he thought about his kids; he tried to keep it ganster, but his heart felt like it was going to explode. And then it happened, the tears raced down his cheeks; it hurt him real bad. He knew little about the circumstances behind the shooting, but it hurt bad all the same.

Reluctantly, he went to the meeting. When Ray walked in the door, he didn't know what to expect, so he decided he was just going to watch and listen to see if he was feeling what the doctor was trying to accomplish through his methods. As soon as he walked in the room he saw his two boys. They didn't speak, just nodded their heads at each other. There was a little bit of chatter going on with the dudes who attended meetings regularly. They were mostly talking about the last meeting, telling jokes about their baby mommas, and laughing their asses off.

Dr. Sampson walked into the room and everything got quiet. "Good evening 'gentle' 'man', putting emphasis on gentlemen being cut into two words. Breaking the word down psychologically set the atmosphere for a calm zone. Dr. Sampson first welcomed all the new comers and congratulated all to the regulars on another week of self-improvement and stress-free living from Baby Momma Drama. He then went on to explain exactly what this group is designed for and the benefits that come from it. It was designed to give men who have suffered from either BM Drama or domestic violence, or *both*, an outlet for release, a chance to see that they are not the only ones going through these situations.

Dr. Sampson started these meetings to enlighten men on the laws dealing with these issues and to share some techniques to help defuse a potential problem from occurring before it starts, and to expose some of the dirty and nasty games that women of all ethnic groups sometimes play in order to control or destroy a man.

Ray was impressed right from the door; he knew this might be something he would enjoy.

Doc continued, "We also take into consideration the health problems that may occur just from the stress, pressure, and anxiety from baby momma syndrome." He also noted that some of these cases have resulted in the imprisonment, destruction, and even death of many, many men. As soon as the words fell off the Doctor's lips, Ray bent over and dropped his face into his hands to hide his tears. The doctor did not know Ray at all and did not know why he had reacted the way he did, he could only assume that he might be an emotional case.

After giving the opening presentation, he asked if the visitors would introduce themselves by their first name and told the new comers that they were free to share if they wanted to. The words that hit Ray's ears rang true and he liked what he heard so far, but he felt like he was in a cross between church and **A.A.** The very thought made Ray laugh a little. "Hi. I'm Ray and I have a problem" Ray started. The room got silent and everybody looked at him. Ray felt a little awkward because of the unwanted attention. The doc realized how Ray must have felt since it was his first time there and all eyes were on him. Doc quickly intervened using one of the techniques he teaches to reverse the situation; bringing the focus to him and off of Ray by making a crazy outburst that made everyone laugh and look at him.

Doc then had everyone get on the same page by having them close their eyes and create a calm and peaceful place to visit in their mind. He then advised them to just relax for few minutes in order to calm the body and free the mind completely before continuing with the exercise.

After about five minutes of complete silence, doc hit two remote controls at the same time and in a split second, the sound proof room went black. Then the very strategically place speakers exploded with some crazy heavy metal music that roared through the room for about forty seconds.

Ray dropped to the floor, crawled back to the wall, and had his hands in a ready to defend position. Randy had a curious, *what the hell is going on,* look on his face. The other two new guys were scared half-to-death as well. When the lights came on, Ray was the first one to speak, "What kind of fucking, crazy shit you got going on down here?"

"Relax Ray," Doc replied. "It's part to us getting to know one another very quickly."

Ray said, "What the fuck is that supposed to mean?"

Doc said, "I've already learned a whole hell of a lot

about you new gentlemen, and if you can be honest, I can prove it."

"What could you have learned about me in less than fifteen minutes?"

"If you really want to know, I will tell you. But, you have to be honest and tell me if I'm right. Then I will take it a step beyond and tell you exactly how I operate and exactly why this support group was started. I must tell you that I only break this entire story down once every three months, but there is something about you that is making me break the cycle. My story is very serious and heart breaking, but first, I'm going to tell you what I learned about you and you will see how real I am. Are you ready, Ray?" The calm and strength that was in the Doc's voice had Ray's full attention.

For a minute, Ray felt fear grip his whole body. Then Ray raised his guard, but was curious about what the doc thought he learned about him. With his eyebrow raised, Ray said, "Yeah, I'm ready," like he was ready to go to war.

So, the doc asked Ray a question first, "Who are you at war with?" Ray curious expression turned to a surprised one. Ray didn't even want to answer, and then the doc said, "You're an aggressive person with a quick temper and a bad one at that. Your mood can change very quickly, depending on your surroundings; which also tells me that you adapt and adjust. Something that was said earlier in this room touched your heart and pulled a tear from you eye; so that shows you do have functioning emotions, which if I may add, is fine. When the lights went out, your actions were that of survival and you expressions were fearless; that showed that you have instinct and courage. Ray, am I remotely close to your characteristics?"

Ray sat there with a look of shock and amazement and

held a new respect for the doc. Ray answered honestly, "Yes Doc. You hit the nail right on the head. How could you see so much in such little time, Doc? What are you, a psychic or something?"

The men all laughed a little. "No, Ray. Quite the contrary. I happen to be a very educated man; I just look like this. Throughout my years, I have witnessed and dealt with many types of problems, directly or indirectly, that pop up at any given moment. So, I learned a lot through life's lessons, even from others, simply because I wanted to learn what makes people do some of the things they do. I also have a few degrees in human behavior, psychology, and human development. So, I watch, live and learn; which become the basis of our discussions. Now that I gave you some of your strengths, I will tell you your soft spots as well.

Ray looked up and started to speak, but doc cut him off and said, "I'll narrow it down to just one, okay?"

Relieved, Ray responded, "Okay."

"You react very quickly without thinking."

Silence fell over the room, and then Ray said, "You're right.

Randy and Harry were in awe; they never saw Ray this humble.

Doc said, "Gentlemen, I just keep it real. Find the truth and look at the entire picture."

CHAPTER TEN

FAMILY GUIDANCE

The Doc continued, "There is a reason for everything, and people put themselves in different positions. You just have to watch the positions you put yourself in, and when you make a mistake, it is okay. Everyone makes errors in judgment, whether they want to be real with themselves or not. Just make sure that if you make a mistake that you learn from it. Then, if you want to take it to the next level, try to help someone else from making the same mistake."

Ray could not believe how interested he was in what the Doc was saying. All he knew was that what was said was some real shit. The Doc said, "Okay, now that you see a little bit of what we are trying to do, let us get started gentleman. Who wants to start?" Ray sat back to observe the next part of the session. One-by-one, men started expressing their pain in stories almost unbelievable. Stories of men put in jail for lies by their ex-wives and baby mommas. Men denied their legal visitation privileges even after fulfilling their part of a court order; men shot and stabbed because of BM drama; men who lost businesses because of BM drama; men who were extorted in court; men who had relationships with their children destroyed because of the lies and actions of their baby mommas. There was one story that stuck out for Ray. One guy was a self-made millionaire until he met his ex-wife. He owned a very successful men's store in Atlanta, which catered to the stars. He always found himself having sex with different broads, sometime two-to-three every week, and on occasion, with prostitutes. He had a lady friend who he never slept with, who he trusted and talked to about everything.

His conscience was bothering him one day, while having a conversation with the lady friend, and he told her he was not happy with the way his life was going, and that he decided he was going to church to try to straighten out his life. She had a friend she wanted him to meet, but once they arrived there, he was interested in someone else. She seemed like a nice woman, you know, active in the church committees, on the choir, and quiet as kept, but full of the devil on the down-low. But this guy, Roger, he was keeper, so she had to put the disguise on. If he knew she was a hoe early in the game, she would not have stood a chance. Her daddy said, "You have to get that one baby. That nigga has money," and "You have to move quickly before someone else snatches him up. I saw that roving eye of his. That boy is on the radio, television, and I heard he is generous with donations." Not only did Roger not know she was a hoe, she put on an academy award winning performance, and swept that nigga off his feet. She stroked his little ego and treated that fool like a king. It was fucked up the way Roger explained it because this gullible, dumb-ass nigga told this bitch all he wanted to do was fall in love.

That boy did not have a clue about whom he was talking to or about the trap that was being set for his dumb ass. He gave her all the ammunition she needed, and his life would change forever.

Six weeks after they met, she was pregnant. Eight weeks after they met, they were engaged to be married. So, now her father could breathe easy; he didn't have to worry so much about paying back the money he borrowed from the Russian Mafia. He was seven thousand dollars behind and they started applying pressure by sending messages.

It got to the point that they were sending a collector to church to collect the collection plate. Her daddy was getting desperate; the church could not have any more services than they already had. They sold so many cakes and chicken dinners that the whole church now has cavities, high cholesterol, and high blood pressure. When he soaked all the money from the church, he would give freely to his unknown, blind cause. They also used all the fixing this and that money from the church to pay his debts, and nothing was getting fixed.

Then Roger's ex had their son, li'l Roger, so that took more money from her father. Her daddy advised her, "Take the sex away from him, make him pay for it or they will kill me."

She said, "Daddy, that's old. Besides, I have been doing that and it does not work any more. All he cares about is his li'l Prince. His pockets got real tight after he was born."

Everyone in the room was completely quiet. If you could have seen the expression on this dude's face while he was telling his story; it fucked everyone up who was in the room. Ray thought, *dam, I thought I was the only one going through bullshit like that!* Roger regained his composure and continued, "She started trying to play mind games". By then, Roger had found out about the graveyard that was hiding in his wife's closet. But he knew she really had him by the balls with the marriage certificate, and the fact that there was child involved; the child who gave him the love that he longed for, for so very long.

After seeing that, Roger became numb to all the tricks and games the bitch ran on him. She had no other choice but come halfway clean, only to the point where she told him all the money she's been spending was to try to help her father out, but it was too late. One of the members of the church, who was close to the family for years, watched her father use and take advantage of people for years, but when they did it to him personally, he felt and looked at them very differently. They straight beat him for twenty-five thousand dollars, and he vowed revenge. He started off with telling Roger everything he knew about the plot that was set against him from his initial conversation with the preacher's daughter. He also told of some other vicious actions that they had done to others just to warn him of the potential danger he could face.

Roger knew at that particular time that the woman's whole family was dysfunctional, even a little retarded, but he did not understand just how desperate and crazy they would get.

Roger said this bitch would physically abuse his son to the point where the kid had to be hospitalized on numerous occasions. Then he said the bitch would call him to let him know. It would usually go down like this: "Well, Li'l Roger fell down the steps again and broke his wrist," or sprained his ankle. And it always happened right after Roger told her she could not have any extra money.

Then he heard a chilling story from his son. Li'l Roger happily asked his Pop if he was going to die. Big Roger said, with a startled and shocked voice, "What are you talking about June Bug?" Little man said, "I thought people cry when people die, but Pop-Pop was excited when him and mommy was practicing their story for the police". The stranger said his son was seven-years old when his son told him that and they were on a supervised visit. That was the only way he could see his son. And the supervision was real tight. He said Li'l Roger's mother did these types of things because she knew how much the little boy meant to his father and she would stop at nothing to crush him, even plotting Roger's death in front of his son, thinking the kid did not understand what was being discussed. So, Roger said he did not push shortie for any more information because he figured that bitch might kill the little boy, too. And, she told so many lies in court, accompanied by political power, and her father had made it impossible for him to try to do anything. Now Roger's living in a strange city, under an assumed name, and paranoid of everyone; most importantly, afraid for his son. He could not keep contact with his son because then they could track were he was, but he couldn't afford the money she demanded and he couldn't' take hearing any more accident reports about his child.

The man ended by saying it took a lot for him to tell his story to the group, but hearing someone else's story helped him get his life back on track, so he hoped to do the same for someone else.

Then Dr. Sampson broke in for a quick minute and said, "That is what this whole session is all about for the new comers." Then he sat back real quiet with his eyes closed.

Ray couldn't believe the vicious story he just heard, but it let him know that he has to be real careful how he handles that bitch, Jackie, after the news he received on the way to the session. Then hearing this shit had him fucked up in the game. One thing he found out for sure was he was not the only one going through it, and these problems could hit any man. So, don't stop.

Everything and everyone got quiet again. All around the room cats were feeling this brother's pain. A couple people thought, *Dam! How could he fall into some bullshit like that?*

Right then, Dr. Sampson spoke again, but very briefly. In a soft voice, he verbalized what most of the men were thinking, "Some of you might think, 'How did he get caught like that?' The answer is easy. It could happen to any one of us, that's how." Then he got quiet again. I guess the reality of what was being said could be felt around the

211

room and I know everyone was examining themselves; they all just had that look on their faces, like '*dam! I thought my shit was fucked up*'. After about five minutes of complete silence, Dr. Sampson asked if anyone else wanted to share before he proceeded.

Another brother, about thirty-eight years old, spoke out. "My name is Maurice and I am very proud and inspired that this brother made it through that fiery clip of his life. I'm also glad that you chose to face your situation, as well as to identify it in this manner, rather than becoming a statistic like so many of our brothers. They end up trapped because of the lack of understanding that should have been instilled in them as young men. By sharing your story, you help yourself and many that hear you, in more ways than one." Maurice continued, "I just wanted to get that off my chest before I went any further."

Ray was extremely impressed with the fancy words the obviously well educated Negro used. He could not believe, based on this dude's appearance, that he too had BM drama. He looked like some kind of administrator or executive for a company. And you know fancy-dressed people are not your candidates for this type of bullship; so people may think…people like Ray.

Because of his attitude, class, and demeanor, he was a very interesting character; one worth listening to, if nothing else.

Maurice continued, "There should be more programs set up like this world-wide. This problem spans the world and someone needs to warn young black men, and teach them about these problems. This type of drama could potentially walk into their lives if they allow themselves to be placed in the positions we found ourselves. I know this from experience; I was one of those young boys."

CHAPTER ELEVEN

THOSE THAT ARE CLOSEST TO YOU STICK THE KKNIFE IN YOU THE DEEPEST!!!!!!!!

I was at the building one day with my landlord hat on, ya dig! My cell started playing "Tupac's, how do you want it", I answer the phone what' really good! I get the voice on the other end talking about, what's up with them books don't make me have to take your ass to court! I immediately exploded, who the fuck is this bringing scared business to my phone? The nigga replied oh you don't know who it is now? I caught his voice, but I was puzzled by the comment, cause I didn't know what the fuck cuz was tripping on, but that court shit don't sound right in my ear, that's the type of shit that bitches and bitch-ass nigga's do cause this bull-shit with him definitely should not have gone down no how no way, but damn if old-boy cat ain't going to get to the bottom of this bull-shit! So I asked this chump what the fuck he was talking about, the nigga said his brother called him from Maryland and told him the book was out, he seen it on line! I computer quickly scanned, broke down, and processed the whole situation in less than 30 seconds, and I just said wow! I couldn't believe a poisonous dart could travel that far and penetrate that hard! This man didn't have a penny invested in this project I was letting him in on, I'm doing something for him people don't do for niggas! I asked him how did we end up in court, I told that chump he's worst than my babymomma! This nigga didn't keep one meeting we were suppose to have, never returned any of my calls and the only time we linked is when I stopped at his job! I should've known some bull-shit was brewing one day his brother called me out the clear blue, I'm thinking maybe this nigga going to send me some of that money he stole a couple years ago, but instead he came out of left field with I heard my brother is writing a book for you! I said what, where did you get that from? I said naw cuz it ain't really none of your business, but I'm publishing some work with mine to get his name out there, but I was expecting our conversation to be about that cheese you owe me not about what me and your brother is doing! After I check this nigga and put him in his motherfucking place he don't want to talk no more, so I guest the cross was in ever since then, I just never thought this nigga would do no shit like that, but I learned that even your own family might pray for your down fall. This nigga nver called my phone when he was suppose to, but called me immediately on some bull-shit! After I got finished with cuz he felt like a pile of shit, as he should cause I keep asking him what the fuck we going to court for cause the only times I went to court is when these crackers locked me up with dams near 20 years for something I didn't do and when this bitch dragged me into court on some extortion- shit, now where do you fall in at homie! This chump said to see if the book is out, I already knew what it was and how I was going to handle it I just wanted him to see what he looks like to me now! After the nigga apologized and all the other shit niggas try when they know they done fucked up for real! I calmly told cuz I'm still going to publish my book I'm just going to take his shit out, I told the nigga he set me back a couple months but I'm glad his true colors came out before I paid all that money to get the book out, cause remember he was and is still broke, but his work was right in this section, so I replaced it with some real shit that could keep you from experience some shit like this, cause I 'm not going to lie it does hurt a little bit!

Finally after all this time, years done went by and I had to be patient before releasing my next project, I had to straighten out a lot of problems that arose after a nigga started seeing some good cheddar. I had people asking for favors that I never knew cared about me, especially when I was rotting away in that funky ass prison caged up like some kind of animal or something, no visits, no food packages, money orders, not even a letter. but they want to talk to me about something real important now, hah! I guess when I was at my lowest point in my life I didn't need nobody right. I could never forget what I went through, cause that's what molded me into the man I am today, and that I wouldn't change for nothing in the world cause I love the way I get down, shit I know I came a long way from busting techs on blocks! I worked very smart over the last few years to gain my current position, and I had to dip and dodge a lot of bullshit along the way, and I definitely paid the cost to be the Boss and floss this hard, now we going to have some fun, "let's go"!

I had to sit down and think about how to come at little bra, cause right now It's a real critical time in my life. I mean, I got all kinds of shit coming at me, unfinished work and projects and I'm giving it everything I got and I've obtained the best position I ever had in life in spite of the land mines I was forced to survive, all of attacks I had to sustain, battle and beat down, and I mean they was coming from everywhere and it's not like he don't know about all this shit. And I don't ask him for much, but damn sometime I got my eyebrow up on this nigga. He knows on top of everything else my wife is another story.

215

When I'm forced to look down the line for the future and well being of my family this man is in that plan, and he know I'm always in his corner and to be real he always comes threw by the end of the day. I guess we have this little talk every six months or so, maybe I'm bugging out! But that's my nigga!

This guy is making checkers moves with a chess master foolish kid, unfortunately for him I've had much worst tried by much smarter and greasier haters than him. But I'm so sharp and smooth with mine I just side step you little monkeys, laugh at the week ass game ya'll come at me with, let that weak bullshit slide off my back like water off a ducks ass, and keep it moving on you broke-ass busters, shining like the sun. But ya'll ain't the only ones, believe me, family, so called friends to nigga's like u who know nothing at all about a nigga like me, except he's a fly motherfucker. And on the real you want to be me. You want to drive all my cars, rock this fresh ass wardrobe of mine, the minks, all that ice you want it all don't u nigga! And I did that with out busting a sweat," motherfucker can u do that"? I hope u can cause that the only way you going to get it, but I doubt it, most haters are not the sharpest ginzu on the chopping block ya dig! And definitely won't get none of that good shit trying to count my money, shit I have a hard enough time trying to keep up with all this shit my damn self, and I know everywhere it's coming from. Right now I'm cool but if I need help counting I'll let ya'll know, but I'm not making no promises o k., but don't hold ya breath nigga!

This is only a few of the small problems that slowed me down from getting back to my readers, but I cleared all of that shit up, and I mean all of that shit up but I got they ass now in a choke hold and I ain't letting them go! Shit I know they mad but I'ma do it like Jay I'm gonna rock more ice and more Versace, Ya'll know the rest.

Chapter Twelve

Session two

(Dr. Sampson took it to the next level and set up an on-line counseling session just like they have online college courses, Immediately the emails started pouring in. It was an instant success and a very smart move on Dr. Sampson's behalf. To make himself available globally to men around the world was an ingenious idea on his behalf)

Check out the emails that were pouring in:

Pete write's in from Detroit:
Years ago when I went down on that bike my whole way of thinking changed drastically, security for my family weighed heavy on my mind constantly. I would never want my wife and kids to ever forfeit any of the living luxuries that they have been enjoying since I came home from the penitentiary, and why should they, shit I'm a real nigga, ya dig! Now I already knew I couldn't get an insurance policy cause I was a convicted felon, so I had to use unorthodox measures to financially protect mines, so I had to come up with some real live and high powered shit, cause my wife can't go through no more struggling not if I can do anything about it! So my wheels started Turing, creative juices get to flowing and old boy Cat came up with a bulletproof plan. Now after evaluating the entire situation I knew I had a tall order in front of me but I knew I was built like that, ya dig!
Joe Write's in from Canada:
When I sit back and ponder over all the bull-shit I been through every since this gold-digger went on the

hunt for the money, I must admit I made the shit look easy, like a walk in a park on Sunday morning, and that's on my momma, and never missed a payment. Chicken thought she was going to stop the kid imagine that! Bitch must not've been listing when her buddy the judge saluted a nigga. I'm mean I really had to put my hustle game down. Alright check it out, I have family and good friends everywhere, so all I did was make them business offers they would be stupid to refuse. I set up L.L.C. Companies in five different states, I fronted the money, put together the business plan, controlled and had access to all the money for all the companies and I mean everything is to legit perfectly legal and ain't a damn thing my babymomma or her gay ass boyfriend can do about it. Now let me see u tell the judge that shit right there b-och! I know ya'll trying to find out where the cheese is at, but I ain't telling u, or your faggot-ass boy friend, I told u I was insulated against you, and I knew I was going to have to do it like that dealing with a chicken like u, believe me I know your kind and I know what type of wickedness u are Capable of, so I hope u understand why I had to protect myself from people like you. Oh f.y.I. You never got one dime from me not one fucken dime, and your bitch-ass boy friend wish he could lay in the bed and touch the type of paper I fuck with. I play with the type of cheddar that nigga dreams about, trust me. And everything he wishes he could do, I did it two maybe three times. This faggot wishes he had a house, nigga I had 20 at one time and u trying to get one. Nigga I got stores, bars, restaurants, and property in other states and countries, and I know you ain't smart enough to do some shit like that from talking to you retarded ass one time, but believe me she would've took anybody who wanted her so as long as u do what the fuck she tell u to do, your broke ass should be alright, so enjoy your free ride sucker, but remember you could never fill my shoes kid, you definitely not built like this nigga, "this shit takes years of experience and bottles of Becks beer chump!

Fareed writes in from London:

I never trip on any of their tactics of their very cause. I already knew I'm way smarter than their entire counsel put together, I mean shit even the judge told that chicken that I was a very intelligent man, but I guess she was so bitter, jealous and envious that the words went right over her head. But at least the judge recognized the moved a nigga was making, but at the same time he was hot cause he couldn't trace all that trap he knew a nigga was capable of making. But be real who in their right mind would give the enemy, info to attack them with. I mean its not like I don't know how vicious she could be, and I know how jealous she is of my wife, cause she asked me how the fuck I'm going to buy her another house and a knew car? I couldn't believe she had the nerve to ask me some bullshit like that after everything she put me through, I simply replied that's my wifey she can get anything she wants first of all! Now when u become a wife maybe your nigga might be able to get u some of these benefits that my wife enjoys, I doubt it very seriously that it will be the same as my wife got it, but it'll be better than nothing, but please don't try and compare yourself to my wife cause Its to different leagues and that's a league your way out of.

Raheem writes in from Detroit:

I was just minding my own b I and all of a sudden out of no where here come a blast of jealousy, envy, and strife like I never seen before. My b.m. Called me one day asking me why I didn't tell her that I Opened my own store, like I'm suppose to report to her like she's the I.R.S. or something. I paused for a minute cause I

219

couldn't believe the nerve of this broad, I keep my cool and calmly asked her if she received her child support check her boyfriend was so concerned about last week. That chicken went crazy on that phone, motherfucker the papers are in the mail! I said, what u call yourself threatening me, bitch my money is insulated against you. It didn't take long for it to register what insulated meant, but this chicken ask me, check this shit out, "how the fuck u going to buy her another key word "another" house and car, shit every thing she got should be mine". I was like where do u get some bullshit thinking like that. Did u forget the shit you did after that u had to know we could never be together. Then u brainwashed my kids, turn them against me, and now u concerned about my chips, what I drive, how I live, all the beautiful gifts and vacation around the word wifey enjoys, I just don't see where u get this type of foolishness from. Then out of all your baby-daddy's I'm the only one in spite of all the bullshit u put me though not only am I the only one who pays support I also help u with their shoes and school clothes, but I bet you'll never tell nobody about that, and as part of the control, and manipulation process I know u didn't tell my kids it came from me! As a matter of fact I bet u even gassed it up a little, just cause I know what your capable of. And   I have a lot of grinds and family and I hear the stories and I been to court to see the type of tactics these hold digging hoes are using these days. So after what u have said and done to me I could only imagine what u told mines about me. But the blood test showed who the liar was, is, and always will be. But that's what jealousy will do for a person, I know u thought I wasn't going to be shit my whole life, and I know for a fact u never thought I would be doing like this, but your not the only one. You thought everything was a joke when I was in the process of getting my life in order when I was driving the little beat up Renault alliance, remember what u said with your little chuckle," I see u in your lexis. Now after about a 25 car up grade now u want to get in a pimps pocket u and your new man. I got one thing to say "Get Your Hand Out My Pocket NIGGA!" I should be writing at least 4 pages a day to catch up with my work, but every time I look up it's something else. I guess If it comes my way I must be able to figure it out someday somehow, cause I'm built like that man! I just get to dipping and slipping, bobbing and weaving something like pretty-boy Floyd and always end up working it out somehow.

Maurice write's in from Atlanta:

So much shit done gone down since my last entry. I past my fire inspection, been In my camera game, caught up with a gang of bills, went and briefed my lawyer on all documents I've obtained pertaining to our up coming day in court with these busters wording about my assets, what kind of cars I drive how many properties I own do I have any other source of Income I mean this nigga act like I owe him something. Now it's bad when a man has a disgruntle ex he has to deal with, but her husband. What the fuck type of nigga does some bullshit like that. I mean you kind of expect that from a jealous bitch that's on the outside looking in, but really they're not even looking they're more like ear hustling and investigating cause I don't fuck with them busters like that. But a nigga counting another dude's money, that's shit broads do. So I guess his mind set is that of a woman, which makes him a bitch ass nigga. I mean this nigga act like he wrote a piece of my book or maybe he helped me flip a couple of them cribs I done sold, or maybe the nigga thought he help close a few of them six figure deals. Or maybe he though he held the camera during a video or movie shoot. This nigga act like he was on the site banging nails when we was building one of these cribs we done sold. Only thing is I never seen him anywhere, so I can't figure out how he got his panties up in a bunch? I was always told by real nigga's that you never count the next mans money, get your own.

Ralphwritesinfrom Chicago (He'sabouttokillhisbitch):

These sore losers wanted to go to court cause they found out about some property I had for about seven years that I didn't tell them about, now tell me that's not some funny shit! So we go to court and I was upset cause these busters trying to get a pimp locked the fuck up and that's not a place for a nigga like me. I said oh hell no it's time to put a stop to this bullshit right now. It's time to introduce you side busters to Mr. Rich Goldstein attorney of law, cause u Negros done got a little beside your motherfucken selves, and I'm going to shut this shit down immediately, cause ya'll got the game completely twisted. Shit I knew I was over paying your dumb ass for the last five years. I let that go for my girls. But your stupid ass want to be greedy moving on orders from your lame-ass nigga, so since u chose court let's get there.

Pete writes in from Atlanta:

Here I am back in a court room again on some straight bull-shit! The inspectors put the heat on the kid about some work that I was getting done at my rest, my people I had working for me started spinning, I had three prior court dates for some other shit I had to get right, can you dig it? But I got the work finished, but since I was late that was an opportunity for the city to come up, so this time they got me! That type of shit right there will teach you to handle your business pronto!

Nicholi writes in from Russia (he's about to kill his bitch too!):

I was reminiscing one day about the start of

my writing career, and all I could do was smile, I mean the planning and execution of all the events that went down was truly amazing and I can't wait to do it again real soon. The trip Texas for the black writers conference alliance, out of this world experience very informative and powerful! I got a wealth of info that I definitely could, did, and will use in the very near future. I took a course on how to self- publish, how to promote, and how to turn your book into a movie on a shoe string   budget, I've been on my shit every since, and that's on my momma It's just everybody else is on the bull-shit, I said can you dig it? But I know how to handle them busters, I feed them with a sling-shot, ya dig, from across the street, and around the corner with ever way it has to go just stay the fuck away from me, shit when they said that the ones closest stick the blade in you the deepest they we're not bullshiting with ya!

Cat writes in from Jersey:
These chickens are crazy out here these days, I mean shit they think if they got a kid by you they can dictate you life, well I know they'll try even by the court system if necessary, trying to find out what a nigga got, how many bank accounts do ya have, telling the judge about what ya heard. Wondering about the kind of food a nigga eat, when you already know a nigga still eating that steak and lobster every week for the last 21 years, so why should it be any different! And I know the last time you tasted that Good shit was when I introduced you to a small piece of that good life, but you know you fucked all that up forever a long time ago, and it ain't my fault your punk-ass boyfriend won't buy it for you but he's doing the very best he can do. And I know you tired of being cramped up in that appartment 14 deep, but that's the life you chose, and I know you found out that I have a couple

cars, business, and property all over the globe, but I didn't build any of that with you lady, as a matter of fact it didn't take me long to figure out that I couldn't even build a trust relationship with a lying bitch like you I knew a person like you could never be trusted ever! So I did what I knew was diffenitly the only thing for me to do and that was get the fuck away from you vicious ass nigga's. And I'm so glad I did, cause if I would of stayed with your monkey ass It would of been like running on a treadmill, going no where running in place. Shit in 19 years you ain't move five miles, I bounced on your scandalous ass and moved 2.8 million miles, I hope I didn't go over your head with that one, and this punk-ass nigga gone tell me he's trying to figure out why all your baby's dads left you? I looked at this retarded motherfucker, grinned and said to myself now if his dumb ass stay around long enough surely he will find out, but I know for damb sure I did the very best thing in the world for me by getting far away from this nasty bitch right here! Shit all I got to do is look at where I made it to and see where she still at and I know for a fact with out a shadow of a doubt I made the right move, cause I couldn't see me with none of the shit I've obtained with a bitch like her, her man can't see him with it neither he's just in denial right now, but in about three years if he's still around he'll know that's as far as they're going! This fool ass nigga talking about every time he ask her about her past she shuts down and cries, gets real sad, shit with a past like that all you can do is cry, and she damn sure ain't going to tell you about that, shit that's why all them other nigga's left they couldn't believe the shit they was finding out about their girl any certain shit no real man can call something like that his woman, so they got the fuck out of there too! Shit your dumb ass is the only one who wants her and she knows that dog, do you honestly think that she's going to answer any of those questions about that grave yard in her closet, the answer dummie is hell no, so take them tears as like it was just to bad to relive, and believe me them Philly-boys help you out while you were gone. You know that old saying you can't teach a old dog knew tricks, and a leopard don't change his spots, I think you know where I'm going with this right, damn I almost forgot what level I 'm dealing with my bad little nigga! But after you read a couple more books you might get a little sharper, I mean shit you can't stay like that forever, or are you comfortable like that? Silly, foolish child!

Sincerely written for you,
Cat

Chapter twelve

Dr. Sampson quickly realized that this was a nation wide problem that definitely needed to be addressed and resolved for the future of the black family. 30 SECONDS OF PLEASURE CAN CAUSE YOU A LIFETIME OF PAIN AND 18 YEARS OF PAYMENTS BELIEVE THAT!

"Everything started out all good. We got along real good and the sex was hot and off the chain. She was the first woman to ever fuck me the way I wanted it, never complaining when it came to that. She was real sweet and could cook; she always wanted to be around me. I should have known that bitch was fatal attraction right then and there!

He was big on the broad and the whole shit, but he really knew she was a lot more serious than he was. I mean, he was only nineteen at the time. The pussy was good and everything, but this bitch was talking marriage. Little did he know, she also had a plan. She told him that she was on the pill, and like a dummy, he believed her. She got pregnant refused to have an abortion. He was not ready to provide for a child and he knew it, but she figured having a baby would secure their relationship, or at least give her enough time to try to make him marry her. However, the more Marvin was around her, the crazier this bitch seemed. She had multiple personalities, which could not be explained because she didn't drink or do drugs. But, at the drop of a dime she could transform into a totally different person.

She was also very jealous and possessive and loved to start fights. After counseling, church, all of the court appearances, and lies to the police, Marvin decided that enough was enough. Their relationship was not healthy at all and was going nowhere. It was like they were from two different places. The only good thing they had was sex, and that shit got old real fuckin' quick when she tried to use sex to control him. He told that bitch the pussy is good, but it ain't that fuckin' good. So that was pretty much the beginning of the end.

That's when he had to keep it real with himself and make one of the hardest decisions he would ever have to make. He had to look into his daughter's eyes and tell her that daddy wouldn't be living with her anymore. She was only two-years old at the time, but it seemed almost like she knew what he was saying. She looked at him with sad eyes and he broke down and started crying. He held her real close to his chest and the thought of waking up and not seeing her little face had him fucked up.

So, Marvin decided that he would live in misery just to be with his daughter. He said to himself, "*I'll just ignore the bitch*". But two weeks later, after coming home from work early, he saw her butt-ass naked, sucking his brother's dick! He couldn't ignore that!

Marvin wanted to kill both of them, but she was definitely not worth doing any time over, at all. So he left. He didn't want to deal with her in the least bit, but he knew he would have to, just to see his daughter.

Marvin knew she had some whorish ways, but dam... his brother! He didn't even want to see him. But now he was wondering how long they had been fucking. Now, I'm not going to sit here and tell ya'll that the shit didn't hurt, 'cause I would be lying my ass off, and that's really the type of shit that would make somebody kill a motherfucker. And to be real, Marvin dad to fight to keep the thought out of his head. He went into a slump, started drinking, smoking weed, not wanting to go to work, or do anything. Five or six years flew by and he was stressed out. One day he looked in the mirror to see a beastly looking man, hair all wild, beard looking all crazy and shit. He just sat there looking at himself in the mirror (that was one hell of a look in the mirror), and he said to himself, "*Self, I know you ain't going to let that bitch do you like this. Nigga, shake that shit off and move on, just like life does*".

Brothers", Marvin said with somewhat of a smile on his face, "it was on at the point Marvin said, "You see. I wasn't ever a slouch. As a matter of fact, I used to move a lot of shit on the street. The biggest fence on the street didn't have shit on the drug tip and me. I was straight killing cash. But I had stopped hustling for a couple different reasons. Two of my partners got killed in a drug deal gone bad by some niggas from North Philly. And, this witch popped up pregnant, so I had to chill. But in the process of me taking it down a little, she tried to take me out by using the games that females play, and by any means necessary: from calling the police, to using your child, to fucking your brother.

So, Marvin sat there thinking for a while and he said to himself, *My Momma didn't raise me like this. I know for a fact that I can do much better that this. I want to make my mother smile and be proud of me when my name is mentioned, not look or feel disgusted when her son's name is brought up.* So, he sat all night and thought of a master plan to get on with life and let that nasty miserable bitch live hers; by herself."

Dr. Sampson never said anything the whole time Marvin was talking. Often times, he just sat quietly nodding his head as if to say yes, with his eyes closed and with a pleased look on his face. Marvin paused to take a sip of coffee, smirked a little, looked around and sensed that he had everyone's attention and everyone's interest.

"I decided to straight ignore this simple bitch, just like I allowed myself to love her, I allowed myself to take the feelings away so that it was like she didn't ever exit. So, you know the bullshit with her intensified. I became immune to the bitch. She couldn't understand how focused I was, and she didn't have a clue about what I was trying to accomplish. But to be real she couldn't understand because she was too small-minded. I just kept up with my research and my studies; diligently working hard to obtain my credentials and the knowledge to put my plans into effect. I sacrificed much for greater gain and greater positioning in life, and also to try to be a positive example for my daughter and build something for her. I had no problem moving on, but she was like a gnat that wouldn't die and wouldn't go away. A couple years went by and I tried to love again. I met a very smart and pretty young lady, and I mean, a 'real' woman, not a hood-rat."

Marvin laughed slightly when he described the difference in the two types of women a man could meet. "On one hand, you could meet a gold digger, and on the other hand you could meet a priceless diamond, ready to support a brother, one who is down with him no matter what, unconditionally. I put together a bullet proof business proposal, hollered at a couple old G's from back in the day who I knew had faith in me and were smart enough to give me the help I needed. We started an independent young, black corporation, networking with people around the world. But she didn't know how everything went down, nor did her dumb ass think I would be smart enough to make some of the major moves I was making.

Where she really fucked up was when she failed to give me credit for not thinking about her trying to get in my pocket; and try she did. She didn't have a clue to the way we set business up, which was none of her business anyway, but for some reason this whore thought that because she was the mother of my child, she should be treated like my fiancé. She would say things like, 'Everything you gave her should be mine. Why couldn't you do all this when we was together?' I looked her right in her face and said, "You wouldn't let a man be a man, remember you wanted to be in charge, you crossed me in the worst kind of way and you have the audacity to fix your face to say some shit like that. Bitch, you have lost your mother fuckin' mind. I looked her straight in her eye sockets, as if I was speaking to her soul and said, 'You don't even exist to me. And you are a poor excuse for a woman, and I wish I never met you. The only good thing that came out of us meeting is our little girl, but you use her like a pawn, instead of treating her like a child.'

Marvin said that the picture this chic was lookin at, standing from the outside looking in, was too much to bear. So, she, just like any other jealous, gold-diggin' hoe, started playing the court game. "And that's when she found out she was not going to get what she thought she was going to get. Oh yeah, that was when everything came out. She tried to tell the judge about my business, well…at least what she thought she knew. She mentioned the car wash, the restaurant, the clothing store, and the stocks. She looked real stupid when the judge read the papers and told her all of that was in my cousin's name. She looked like a complete asshole. That could not have happened if I would have married that chicken head. She would have really cleaned me out and the judge would have helped her. Well, she wasn't just going to let everything go like that; oh hell no, not just like that.

After she picked up her welfare check, got down to that hair salon with the rest of the hood rats, and got to gossiping, she was really gassed up. I mean, just the thought of her getting a real weave sown in, instead of the glue, and going to the oriental instead of the school to get those nasty little nails looking like something. Most of the hoochy-mommas feeding this chic didn't like her at all. To be real, they were just trying to make her mad. They would say shit like, 'That fine-ass nigga Marvin; a bitch got to be stupid to let that nigga get away. Shit, the bitch must not have any skills, 'cause he sure knows how to take care of his woman'. Then the rest of them would get started about how he laces his new wife with diamonds, furs, and foreign cars, just because they knew she was listening and she never tasted any of the shit".

Marvin kept smiling while telling his story, and he had everybody in the room a little confused because most of them cringed at the thought of their BM. The brothers were feeling him for real, but they could not understand how he could smile. After a few years of going back and forth to court, Marvin said he got tired of fighting with this broad and getting nowhere. "I mean, put yourself in her shoes; you would be mad too, looking at someone she was fucking and had a child for be successful without her. She never thought I would amount to anything because I didn't have shit when we were together, and now I'm driving a Benz and Limos; I run a business; and I don't give shit. It was obvious that all she wanted was money, and when she heard I had something to do with a movie deal, she threatened to commit suicide; which I thought would be the best case scenario for me, but the worst for my daughter."

Marvin said that he realized that even a dog has to get crumbs off the table sometime, so he decided to throw her a bone. Marvin knew how jealous she really was because he had more than she ever dreamed of. And she knew she would never even be married, let alone own a new car or a house; she really felt left out. But she did it to herself.

He said he took her out to eat so they could talk. He gave her a proposal, indicating what he would give her, but she said she wanted to go through the court before he even finished what he had to say. He told her he had no faith in the court system, and she said that was his problem if she wasn't mistaken.

He told her, "You don't even understand how degrading that is to have some joker play God over another man who already handles his responsibility, especially when there are other fathers out there who really don't give a damn, and the women won't open their mother fuckin' mouth about it. But the good man has a women who wants to give a good nigga a bunch of bullshit." Marvin said he told her he was just trying to keep the peace, it would be better for everybody, and that is the way it should be anyway. "Just because we couldn't make it work doesn't mean our child should have to suffer, 'cause we…well, I know I don't want her to think any of this bullship is her fault. And, I definitely want to be there for her when she needs me, and I'm not just talking about when she wants me to buy her something. You already know I don't let nobody take advantage of me."

Everybody in the room was so deep into this dude's conversation; they were all "kind of zoned out," but they heard every word he said. Ray was kind of shocked because, number one, he felt a little better and he learned something. And, he really didn't expect to hear a story like that and how this dude controlled the situation. He didn't look like he was built like that. But, I guess that is why they say, "Never judge a book by its cover."

Marvin continued, "Now fellows, I don't want ya'll to think that it was just cut and dry to the bone like that. Some chics you can talk to, and some are very unreasonable. I don't want you to think I'm trying to mislead you in any way.

But I knew it was time to talk to this broad because it was ready to get real ugly. Word started spreading like wild fire about this particular movie deal, and she had all types of chickens gassing her up; they had her thinking that she could really get half. And I know how she tried to cut up the last time I made a little noise. So, I knew how bad she craved for some attention or something, and I decided to let her in on a little secret before she started up with the bullshit again. I told her all the checks were legally put in my cousin's name early in the game because I knew how she got down. But if she acts right in spite of all the previous bullshit and if everything goes right, I will break her off something decent. She said, 'You said that the last time,'"

Marvin preceded, "Listen brothers. This is where the problems stem from. I had to let her know that I have to take care of me first; make me happy. My obligation is to my daughter, not her mother, but she tried to take mine so I had to protect myself at all times, just like in boxing.

In my life I saw best friends turn on each other; some sent their best friend to prison for life, and some even murdered their best friend for their own gain. And I'm talking about a woman who can't have you anymore, and there's nothing she could do about it. She is on the outside looking in. She does not know everything that is going on, or the type of moves you had to make to get where you are, or how hard you had to work or all the sacrifices you had to make. But really, she didn't give a fuck, all she knew was it appeared that I was balling and she was not. A man appears to be happy: new wife...new car...new home...trips around the world-three or four times a year…diamonds…furs…limos…and all the good shit. And she's sitting home alone, has to walk to work, has to wear the same busted clothes she was wearing when you left her, with the same ghetto mentality. There's no elevation what so ever, nothing but jealousy and envy for everything you have done and become without her. So, you know what she's going to do, right?

Remember her theory, 'By any means necessary, no matter who gets affected.' I only want you brothers to know what could possibly happen after about forty seconds of pleasure. It could cost you much, not just money; and it could last for many years. So, I encourage you young brothers in here to handle your situation delicately and carefully from here on out. Also, always take your children into consideration first because they didn't ask to come here and they are most important over everybody. You do not want to be the cause of any problems your child might encounter in his or her future. I know some of the games that some woman play are foul and very unnecessary, but trust and believe, when that child gets old enough and finds out the truth for himself, he will know who the real monster is. So, you brothers remember to think first, examine the whole picture before you react and learn the law because you have rights too. But the judge will not tell you what they are, you will have to find them out yourself or hire a lawyer.

A lot of brothers have problems paying child support because of the unbalanced pay scale between white and black employees. But the judge does not care about what you make. What you have to do is put a motion in for a reduction of support and joint custody. That will cut your child support in half. See how she likes it when you start exercising your legal rights.

She wants to cry hardship and wants an increase from you alone, instead of getting an initial support order from all her other children's fathers. Tell the judge you will take the children if that bitch has it so hard. Tell him that she doesn't have to pay anything, and watch how easy her hardship will become. It is not the usual case of the woman really having a hardship; it is just 'you look too happy and comfortable.' The picture that she is only looking at, and not taking part in, is too pretty. Also, it is killing her that she is not the chosen one. You young brothers must know the truth so you can watch the positions you could easily fall into. And, if you are already in this position, maybe now you know why. The kid is all she has to try to hurt you with, and she will use the child in a heartbeat.

Now, some of you cats got superstars and don't even realize it until you lose her and end up with a monster like I did. Yeah, she might try to be a little bossy, and nag a little or a lot, but if she is supportive of you by cooking, cleaning and loving you right, and trying to help make your house a happy home, respect that and respect her. All women are not like that, but be careful because if push comes to shove you will see the shit she can get you into. That is my story. I hope it will help somebody in some way. So, my advice is to think first about your child and the best way to handle your situation after you take everything into consideration. Then make the best decision possible, but always remember if possible, it is cheaper to keep her. Believe that! And, she knows it, so she is in a win-win situation; that is why she pops that shit."

Everything got quiet again for a few minutes, then Dr. Sampson looked at his watch and said," "We're going to end here if there is no one else who would like to speak."

Silence fell around the room and Dr. Sampson said,

"I'm very pleased to see all the new faces. I hope everyone felt comfortable tonight and I want to assure you that it feels different each time you come. We have done a study in many different cities around the world that proved our sessions have been very successful in helping brothers. The sessions have helped men understand why some of these problems are occurring, how some could end, and how to deal with them the best way possible. Ninety-eight percent of the fellows who have attended sessions have openly shared the differences in their lives after light was shed on their darkness and after some education was applied. Once again, we will never pressure you for money or make you feel uncomfortable in any way, and feel free to visit us again. Now, if there is nothing else, I'll say 'Peace' until I see you fellows again."

Some of the guys sat around and kicked it out front. Ray was not with that bullshit right there, but found the session very interesting and said he would go again. Randy and Harry walked up to Ray's car before he pulled off. Ray dropped his window and a big cloud of smoke perfumed the air. Harry said, "Man, that smell like weed."

Ray started laughing and said, "You almost reminded me of Sherlock Holmes with that one, Money!"

Harry said, "I didn't know you smoke marijuana,"

"There's a whole hell of a lot of things you do not know about me, Son. And beside, nobody told you to come running up to my car anyway!" exclaimed Ray.

Harry bitched up right away, "Now Ray, I didn't mean it like that, Fam."

Ray said, "It's cool, Man. I'm just not for that bullshit right now. My mom is not doing too good in the hospital, my lawyer is trying to rip me off, my baby's momma is trying to set me up to do time and get robbed, then

236

today, I find out one of my partners was set up and killed by his Baby mom. So I can't take no more, and I'm ready for whatever. But, yeah dog, I smoke weed every day and now you know why."

Randy was left standing there with his mouth open, yet never uttering a word. For the first time, he tried to put himself in his friend's shoes, and it dam near scared him to death. The very thought of it being him left him totally speechless and teary-eyed.

After the meeting Ray said, "I don't know if this stinkin' bitch really understands what I'm going through. Or, does she even care? That is what I'm left with, Dog. But at least I know I'm not the only one going through the bullshit! Yo, I gotta go check on my momma. Ya'll fools stay up. I'm out!" Ray eased off kind of slow, and then he punched it and took off like a bat out of hell.

Both Randy and Harry saw everything very differently from that point on. Neither one had problems like the ones they heard tonight.

Ray's mind was racing one thousand miles a minute; the continuous thoughts could not be stopped. While driving down the high way, Ray tried to arrange his thought process on a priority basis. He had smooth Jazz playing, which had the power to soothe the savage beast that could rise in any man.

Ray said out loud, "Dam, that white boy is blowing the shit out of that Sax." It all seemed like a dream to Ray when he put all the evening's experiences together. The hardest thing to swallow, besides his mother, was the death of his partner because of Baby Momma Drama!

* * TO BE CONTINUED *

I already know she is mad, shit that hooker told me "everything my wife got should be hers " I knew right then and there, this chic was out of her mother-fucking mind "! But I seen this with chic's many times before and a real nigga will understand that's in the nature of most women, and after they see a nigga balling out of control , not being a part of all that is painful enough, but hearing this shit constantly, everywhere, and from anybody is a killer for sure. And if I wasn't asked why I didn't do all this stuff when we was together, maybe I wouldn't feel this way, but again I seen, and heard worst shit some of these bitches try and do! But when another nigga is acting like that, this is a first! But I even understand that, cause his girl feels like she's slited, cause he know he could never do no shit like what he read, saw, and investigated! I know that chump wish he never tried to find that type of shit out. I had a conversation with his simple ass, and I can imagine this nigga with a calculator working out them numbers,I know that because he told me he read my book while he was down prison, I chuckled a little and said oh yeah, make a long story short,and a short story shorter, this duck-ass nigga, believed a liar from the beginning like she really going to tell him how she really got down back in the day, so you could leave like everybody else, but the nigga said he told here to sue me if it wasn't true. I really couldn't believe what I was hearing from this dude, " I'm laughing to myself saying what the fuck type of nigga is this! Then I said to myself the type of nigga real niggas don't fuck with! So I faded this faggot and kept it moving! So I called a couple of my strong people to let them know what was going down and they wanted to go slap his punk-ass just cause I was up set, and their fist statement was what the fuck he got to do with that if he was a real nigga, he would check her dumb-ass for playing games like that especially if he got kids by somebody else, cause he wouldn't want that shit done to him, I told my dude,"that's the difference between a real nigga and a fake one, cause a real nigga always get's his own money, them haters worry about the next man! So you know he needs a leader. But when I seen that nigga's reaction to the reduction I just smiled, like oh this nigga is really mad, it was so funny! That nigga said out loud "that's some bullshit", I laughed and said he must of really thought he was going to come up! Ha ha, the first time I went to court by my self, only cause I knew we had to come back, but what I knew immediately after seeing how they was going to treat a pimp, and this duck is making smart remarks about every case that went before us and then the visible excitement of my slating, and knowing I've been over paying this chicken ever since she followed your weak ass orders, I knew if we ever had to come back again that's when you dumb- ass will experience the strength of street knowledge, and also meet a couple members of my team! Shit I was on the mic with one of my lawyers, while this chump was smiling and I heard him saying yeah we got your ass now, that was the first time he really verbally invoked himself in my shit, but since we was in court, I was on the phone with my lawyer while I was walking out the court room! This foil ass nigga thought because now after he comes home and finds out the kid got way more than we imagined boo! I think if he got all that he should be giving you x y z! No you stupid motherfucker what you think don't count at all, that's what the judge meant when he told you, if your going to stay in the courtroom you have to shut the fuck up, in other words, mind you fucking B.I. , cause you acting like a hoe that's out of pocket! In street terms you just like a BIOTCH!!! I say can you dig it, "SUCKER"? And you have the balls to invoke you opinion about what a real man is, your simple ass couldn't recognize a real man if he slapped your stupid looking face! But the judge did, peep the questions he asked after he shut your dumb ass down. Now I really was almost convinced that your broad was sincere with the performance she displayed in the courtroom, it almost looked real, but the judge didn't believe that bull shit, and I seen a similar performance before my damn self, nigga you know what I'm talking about, you might be illiterate, but you can't be that fucking stupid, or can you be? Peep what the judge asked her nigga, and we going to let the world judge this shit right here toy faggot! Yeah nigga that's how much power I got nigga, I can check you expose you, read you, your mother-fucking rights, teach your dumb-ass something,clown you, and get paid,all at the same time, MOTHER-FUCKER can you buy that!! You remind me of some snotty little bitch that came up to me when that book that's killing you fist came out. Little chicken came up to me and said I know everything about you, I said no Baby, you only know what I wanted you to know, on a as needed to know basis, but like I said that came from a bitch! And then you had the nerve to tell me that you was trying to figure out why nobody wanted to stay with her, " Playboy said you should ask yourself that question, listen to yourself then think about it real hard before you answer that shit my nigga, cause all them niggas couldn't be wrong, come on now, nobody wanted to stay but you,and I'm not mad at you, you know she used that good increase she Got to hold you Down, my lawyer told me I over paid her 25000 dollars, my highlight was when the judge asked how many other kids she got, and by how many different fathers and who was paying child support, all these other fathers only one man has ever paid support, and your about to have another one by someone else and you want a increase! Shit Ray-Charles and Stevie Wonder could see that bull-shit, and you MADD, my youngens even said what the fuck type of nigga is you, and I told them I ain't never seen no faggot shit like that in my life, but we won and ain't loose a wink of sleep! But I had a ball spending that reduction! Nigga I got me a I-Phone that I'm using to clown your fickle-minded ass on, three pair of gucci sneaks, a WII game and a Jacuzzi, motherfucker can you buy that!!

A WORD FROM Cat Daddy

MEN HAVE RIGHTS, TOO

Yes, there is a financial obligation for the care taking and well being of his child from every man who chose to reproduce. Although every man does not satisfy his responsibilities, all men shouldn't be judge for what some men do. And on the same token, every man should have the right to bond with his child, and not on the mother's terms.

Too many women are exploiting a crooked, system designed to break up the family structure between children and their father, in the hope that she would break the man she didn't know how to keep or treat. And because the man is often comfortable with the separation, a lot of women can't take it when he finds another companion, so they try to use the system any way they can, resulting in extortion tactics governed by the system. She could care less about the man she supposedly loved so much at one time, and she sacrifices her own children's lives for her own plan and purpose.

This letter does not pertain to all women. However, young brothers, be real careful when choosing your mate, because you really won't see her true colors until you try to leave. So, watch yourself! And if you really want to know what the broad is going to be like, go meet her momma, because that's where she got most of her training, if she has any at all.

I remember them prison days like it was yesterday, at the end of my bid, I was in Secaucus, N.J. And I was there with a couple of my homies from the streets. My big bra,

242

Umar kelsey, my man Qwasim, and a couple other cats from our-side you know what I'm talking about! Now dig the twist, some buster from Plainfield N.J. That was down Bordentown youth correctional facilities a.k.a. Gladiator school which is just what the fuck it is, an entire jail of young, wild niggas with a ass whole full of time. A place where at any giving time a riot would break out. Now this clown that called himself Amazing went to barbering school with me. Now this chump had a problem with me cause I believed in the bible.now when we ended up at the transition- house I was there first and I was all over that barber's job like a tailor made suit, ya dig, cause everybody knows the barber's job pay the best in the penitentiary, so soon as I see this buster he asked me what's up with that barber's job? I laughed and said nigga you know I got it that's what's up with it! That nigga was hotter than fish grease! Now I told the boy to get some clippers and get in where he fits in! Shit if you nice can't nobody stop you from getting money, but that's only if you're a real nigga, can you dig it! But since we dealing with the total opposite of a real nigga which is a bitch nigga the route he took was totally different. He went to the police and told them I wasn't doing my job and he deserves to be the barber on the south side. So the police asked me why I'm not going to work? I told him that I go to work every day, go ask the c.o. at the front desk that I have to sign in with! Police asked his colleague do I come to work, the cop told him, yeah and he always cleans up behind himself! Now the police go back to amazing and tell him what was said, this nigga flipped out screaming like a little bitch, taking bout he cuts hair on that side every fucking day! So the boys want to know who clippers he was using? He told them his homie's from his city and called him by his government name. So the young punk done opened up a can of worms for their whole crew! The boys run down on his boy smooth looking for them illegal clippers, but the boy was selling dope in the joint! It was a good thing they didn't find no smack! But just the very situation he was put in I could understand why the kid would be heated, and they was about to fuck the boy amazing up, so this faggot tries to tell the boy smoothe that I told the police on him, these chumps came running down my tear like they was going to role your boy out! My nigga Umar heard the confusion and blacked the fuck out immediately, another cat from Elizabeth N.J. Named Malik-Soldier was my bunkie and he was big on the kid and he knew I didn't fuck with nobody so he wasn't having none of that type of shit right there, then a Spanish boy from Patterson name George was the maintenance man he moved out with a big ass phillips screwdriver like who get it Umar? Needless to say them cats backed down immediately as they should!

CHICKEN HEAD CHECK LIST:

Here are a few things you want to check out to see if you have a "Real Woman" or a "Chicken Head".

If your girl falls under more than two of these categories, you have yourself a full fledged, 100% Chicken Head:

✓ If she tries anything and everything to get you locked up,

✓ If she is constantly trying to get more money, saying, "It's for you children," when you know it's for her hair and nails, you have yourself a Self-Absorbed Chicken,

✓   If she is jealous of your new relationship because she is still alone' Chicken...Chicken...Chicken,

✓   If she tries to attack you new mate; Gangster Chicken!,

✓   If she tries to sabotage your relationship between you and your seed; Ghetto, Nasty Chicken,

✓   And last but not least, if she keeps you tied up with court litigations because she is jealous of what you have worked hard to achieve after you left her dumb ass; my man, you have yourself a Problem Chicken.

SPECIAL THANKS

Very special thanks to:

All of my supporters. I really love ya'll and I appreciate all the real love and support you have given me. Ya'll are the reason I keep going. I try to keep it positive and busy to she my little brothers another way, and to show them what hard work, dedication, and determination can get you.

My wife, Tara and my children for their patience while I was working on these last few projects over the past years. I know it was a great sacrifice, but ya'll know I do not start something and not finish it. But, I'm done now and it is going to get greater later.

My book editor, Renee Irwin, who did an excellent job as an editor and advisor. I appreciate all of your help, expertise, and patience with the project. And I wish you much success in your new job. I also appreciate the genuine love you have for kids in the Pleasantville School system, and I know they do too. People can see the ones who really care; especially the people who need someone to care. Thank you.

My digital editor, Romain Haywood. I thank you for working with me and adding that fire to my first mini-movie, "Ride With Me". One Love.

My web designer, Chris Sibbert; good lookin' with the Web page, Shortie. Your work is off the chain. Thank you for everything you have done for me. You were always there for me. And, if they think I'm playing, all they have to do is look at the book covers and the web page to see you work, right! I wish you the best in school and do not stop working on the video game; you can do it!

My Bro. Michel Davis; Keep doing your thing, Big

Bra.

Don Diva; I love the article you laid out and much success for you family and business.

My Cousins; the ones who are real. Thanks for holding me down when things got rough.

To my writing team; the three of ya'll know what it is and I'm ready. I wish you all much success with your career and dreams. Don't ever let anything or anyone stop you. One Love.

Perspective Magazine; thanks for the exposure. Best wishes with your business.

To all my little Brothers who participated in the D.V.D. project, stay focused and grind until you get where you want to be.

My little Brother, Lamar Smith, stay focused kid.

To my homie who participated in "Exposure". I've shown you what it is; now make it happen.

I also have a multitude of supporters who I know for a fact have mad love for the kid. Trust me when I tell ya'll you don't know what ya'll do to me; I mean it. And, as long as ya'll keep asking, "When's the next book coming out?" I'm going to get it to you. To Hell with the haters!

Last but not least, I would like to thank my family around the world; that is, the ones who have real love, because we do have some phonies among us. Ya'll know I have mad love for all my family and nothing has, or ever will, change. These book and movies will not change me. I'm that same dude; I'm just too smart to be played out or used. And, because I speak about the truth I'm considered an outcast, but I've been called worse behind my back. Get it…behind my back! But I love all ya'll.

A word from the editor:

To Sean: Thanks for keeping it real with the kids of Pleasantville. It was through the school system that you and I became friends and it is through the school system that we both continue to shape lives for the better. Your books are not only an inspiration to the people who read them, but the fact that they are written and not just dreamt, inspires our youth to do something positive with themselves. The books, DVDs, and clothing lines also prove to our kids that they can change how they live and learn from their mistakes.

You are a blessing to the neighborhoods of Pleasantville because every time I called you to talk about one of my students who needed help, you were there; you even told me to give the students your telephone number. When I needed you to speak to a group of kids about second chances, you couldn't get there fast enough. I couldn't end this project without showing MY appreciation of YOU! God bless!

Renee Marie Irwi

"IMAGINE"
By Sean Timberlake

Imagine meeting a woman; she's pretty and real thick, something like a Wendy's milk shake. She's cute in the face and thick in the waist, just like something most men would go for. Imagine a woman who knows how to please a man completely, "when she wants to " and "to get what she wants;" one who will accomplish just that by any means necessary. Imagine waking up and looking at your life from a different angle; looking at the direction you are going in, and trying to see where it will lead you in the next five to ten years. Imagine not liking what you see or not seeing a future at all. Imagine being smart enough to acknowledge that a change must be made, and when you start making a change for the better, the woman comes back into your life, claiming to be pregnant with your child. Imagine being shocked because of the current situation between ya'll (not being together at all), but also being happy because a baby is something you always desired, almost more than life itself. Now it's sad when a young man of 18 years feels he needs to have his own child to know what unconditional true love is really about. Imagine thinking prior to this surprise, reality awakening that it was impossible to make a baby because of a few prior miscarriages and an abortion, which you had no say over. Part of you was destroyed when a decision was made without your input; "Imagine that!" Then imagine how happy one could be with this shocking news that finally, after all the bullshit one could possibly go through, you will have the one thing that really mattered in life.

Then imagine having to make one of the biggest

decisions you ever had to make at this point in your existence; you have to break this news to your "True Love", who has always been there for you.

Imagine all of the decisions that had to be made and made quickly. Then imagine being confused and really not knowing what to do, and asking, "Dam! How did I get in this position?"

Now try to deal with it the best way possible, with every part of you shattering into pieces because you see the hurt and pain you caused in the eyes of your true love. Imagine wishing you could take it back and do it all over again, even if this other woman is about to give it to you. Imagine feeling something different in your stomach and all of a sudden that happiness does not feel the same; you're looking at this bitch with shifty eyes now because you heard possible dates from the doctor that made you think real hard, and I mean real hard!

Now you feel like your true love did when she found out another woman was having your child; a child your true love didn't want and couldn't give you. Nevertheless, it was a very sick feeling, one which no one could enjoy having. Imagine giving this broad the benefit of the doubt, but letting her know that as soon as it is possible you are, without hesitation, getting a blood test. Can you imagine what she must have felt like knowing that you had doubts about the paternity?

Imagine going through all of the ups and downs of a pregnancy with this broad, all the way up to delivery; and as soon as you laid eyes upon the little boy, you knew in your heart that something was not right.

Imagine how desperate she must have felt when she sees your reaction; because all along she knew the truth. What could have been going through her mind to cause her to continue to lie? I mean, real tear swearing on this, that, and the third; anything to try and conceal her secret and keep the deceit alive. Imagine the academy award winning performance she must have put on for me to give her the benefit of the doubt one more time; at least until a D. N. A. test could be performed. Not only did my father show me not to run from my responsibilities, but I really wanted the little boy to be mine. However, I could not, for the life of me, get rid of that feeling in my gut. Imagine waiting six more months after already waiting nine months to find out if you are a daddy or not.

Imagine the amount of sex and how good she tried to make the sex, knowing I wasn't playing about that test. Do you think it was a coincidence she got pregnant again immediately or was it part of a plan from a large, wicked plot?

Imagine how I felt five months later when I finally got that D. N. A. test back and it said there was no way possible that I could be the biological father of this child. Every deceitful act that she had done was made crystal clear; from the acting, to the lies, to everything to give the boy my full name, like he was really Jr. What kind of animal does that? Please tell me!

Imagine finding this out and then the reality that now this bitch might really be having one for me now. Imagine such a person raising your child.

And to think, I just wanted to do the right thing; you know, be there for mine, even through all the bullshit. I mean, I signed my name on the birth certificate and the whole shit, just because I wanted to do the right thing. And, it was all a trick; a wicked and evil plot, purposely and maliciously done. A very harsh and cruel lesson learned early in life; but life waits for no one, and time heals all wounds.

So I move on with a very uneasy excitement and expectancy about my real child; just put yourself in my shoes for a minute. The child is born and after I saw him,

I knew right away he was mine. The difference between the boys at birth was like night and day. Can you imagine her trying to play the sympathetic role at an emotional time; well, she did. But guess what? It didn't work. The nerve of this bullshit. And said some old slick shit…what did she say again? Oh yeah…holding the baby, trying to cause a romantic scene the best way she knew how, she said, "You see what we make when we come together."

I said, "What's this, a Kodak moment or something, Bitch! I ain't trying to hear that shit. You know me, and you don't fuck around like that, not after what you did to me. Shit…your baby daddy still owes money."

Imagine how stupid that bitch felt then. I guess she thought we were going to get back together after I saw my son. Ha! Imagine that! With one last desperate attempt before I left the hospital, she asked me if I was fucking anybody. I just laughed and said, "I got to use the bathroom." I just laughed. "HA!" The nerve of the bitch. Right when I flushed the toilet she burst in the door and grabbed my hands while I was pulling my zipper up, talking about, "Wait a minute," as she sat down on the toilet. She said, "I asked you that for a reason." While she was talking, she was slowly pulling my dick out. I mean…she caught me off guard with this bullshit and my man was already there by the time she got him all the way out. He was standing tall, like a proud soldier, serving in the military. Now I was young, but I wasn't stupid. A blind man could see what she was trying to do. She was stroking my wood and mumbling some bullshit, "I know what I did was wrong, but I love you and I didn't want you to leave, just like I don't want you to go now. You know I can't have sex for six weeks, but if you wasn't fucking nobody I wanted to please you…that's why I asked you that. But I don't care," she said. She started crying, "I love you," and threw the dick in her mouth.

Can you imagine what I was thinking? I thought, "This bitch is good!" Remember I told you she was a good actress—well—she just turned into a desperate actress. But I waited until she was done before I said anything. I guess that was her little way of showing me how much she loved me and what she would do to please me. But, in reality, it showed me the lengths and measures desperate people will go to in order to obtain what ever it is they want. Trust me, she put her all into it; she rocked the mic right. I know she was thinking, "I know this nigga ain't going to leave this." Wrong!

Imagine how she felt over the next month when her little idea didn't work and every time she saw you or ya'll talked, all your attention was on the baby. Of course, all her attention was spent trying to talk about us getting back together, but she was getting nowhere with it. Imagine how stupid she must have felt gunning you down in the hospital bathroom for nothing. Then imagine going through every type of personal problem and injustice that life could throw your way (all due to circumstances beyond your control) on top of this problem and interference from a woman who did you wrong and sabotaged her own relationship with you; all because you were able to get on with your life in spite of all the legal and personal problems that could have been thought of. Then, after all that, this bitch was trying to get in my pocket. Imagine how you would feel if it happened to you, your son, your brother, or someone close to you. That is an ugly picture, isn't it?

Our brothers and sisters need to slow down, think,

and be responsible before making babies with people they really don't know. And trust me, you don't know someone or learn about someone in three or four years because they can play a role to get what they want. Thirty second of pleasure could cause you eighteen years of tribulation.

I can't let this book go without sending a R.I.P. to a host of family members and friends I lost since I put my fist book out. Cousin Mary Burke, Russel Gibbson, Warren Hood,Eddie Stoklin, Derrik Brooks,Tony Jalil Howard,Da Da Harmen,Sam Hunter,Quincy Lemmons,uncle George Timberlake,and aunt Bev Timberlake,Kenyetta Jerkins,aunt Wannetta Rose,aunt Vanessa Timberlake, Derrik Brooks, Ruth Blackmen, Bishop Rueben Smith, Lil Bookie, Lamar Greshum, Ceddrik Jackson, Julian Mr. K o Letterough, if I missed anyone of mine please forgive me for the over sight, Cat!

I want to send a special thanks to my strong people (Philly Will), for all your help in finishing up these projects, you really did the damb thing homie, and I'm blessed to have someone like you to work with, you are a very sharp dude and you know we going to pop more bottles, cop more Gucci, and do plenty more business, ya dig! You know we tackled this project like Batman and Robin! Also my lil homie Chriss a.k.a. Shorty, first congrats are in order twice, on the new baby and for finishing school, now that we got this projects done I guess I'm graduating my damb-self! But when you graduate that means, you had to learn something to successfully complete your course. you sending me that book-cover was like handing me my Degree, I said, (can you dig it) my strong peoples be like (yeah Cat, talk that shit) but you know I ain't new to this, I've been doing this shit for years! also want to thank all my family, and real friends who support ya boy, and all the people who bought the first book, ya really showed me crazy love, but most important you solidified my writing career, cause really I'm not a writer, I'm a hustler homie, and if I can make a job out the shit that came across my path, what you call that, you call that being nice, right? Right! Unless your a hater, cause I know everybody got somebody who has a little of Cat in them, his experience that is. And I loved all my people from around Atlantic county that keep the pressure on me (when's the next book coming out) ya just don't understand everything that I do, that I'm involved with and that comes my way, but ya keep me focused. thanks to lady Dee Rollins for giving me my first radio interview, you gracefully asked me the right questions to open your boy up, but I know you was shocked when the owner of the station told you to get me back on their, cause they never in their history had a response to a interview like that, huh ma? Pattie Friend for placing the book in the N.J. prison system, my first t.v. interview the invitations to be key-note speaker at those prison graduations, you know that meant a lot to me. Can't forget my girls at the banks that I deal with, Tareen, Ann-Marie, Donna,Kim, Angela, Debbie, Pat, my girls at the electric company, the gas co., Senn oil, Magic disposal, Stan, joanne, Lanore, Terri,Bonnie over at state farm insurance, my girl over at the child support building that wild out with me every week when I take my weekly bail money over there, ya keep me going, but I told ya what type a nigga I am, I will take a negative situation Into a positive situation for my bank account, I'm laughing at there foolish attempts all the way to the bank, ha ha ha, no really, I'm laughing in line at the bank! Can't ever forget my brother Shon-don, yeah you boy Catastrophe done did it again, we talk everyday, matter a fact I'll call you when I get done typing homi! Al-Sadiq Banks keep banging bra, Mikel Davis mad love kid you know how we do! Shout out to my homie, Jamil, Tariq, Nazerm,umar, Jalal, Pr. Nasheed, Sheed, Sacrifice, JoJo hold your head kid, Vel I seen how they tried to do you at trial, but shit I wish I had Amy Wiensat when my life was on the line, hold your head kid.missing my uncle Buddy Lucas, spade I got them baby I wish you was here to see this shit, but on my mom I did everything I said I was going to do seven years ago breaking night with you in the game room till the next morning, I miss you uncle.